Arthur Miller's
DEATH OF
A SALESMAN

Joan Thellusson Nourse
Department of English
St. John's University

BARNES
&NOBLE
BOOKS
NEW YORK

CONTENTS

INTRODUCTION

MILLER'S CRAFTSMANSHIP

Most critics today would agree that Arthur Miller's technical proficiency is of a high order. From the time he entered the University of Michigan in the mid-1930s, he has studied and practiced his craft. He won several prizes for his plays at the University and later wrote radio scripts in New York. He especially admired Henrik Ibsen, the great Norwegian master of the "well-made" or tightly constructed play; but he also was familiar with the work of O'Neill, Odets, and Wilder, as well as that of such European experimentalists as Brecht. *All My Sons* (1947), Miller's first drama to receive general acclaim, seemed largely to follow the Ibsen tradition. *Death of a Salesman,* however, produced two years later, handled its material more freely, cleverly using flashbacks to permit startling insights into its hero's psychology. *The Crucible* had a different approach, since to the playwright, the overall political issues were at least as important as the inner workings of any character's mind. Miller used a long, expository first scene as an "overture" to acquaint his audiences with the tense situation in historical Salem. Miller continually varies his style to achieve different effects. Certain of his experiments, of course, are more successful than others. But he has at least consistently demonstrated an enterprising and progressive approach to his craft.

MODERN TRAGIC DRAMA

If Miller is noted for stimulating experiments with technique, he has also been widely discussed as a writer of modern tragedies. In earlier ages, tragic plays had dealt mainly with the overthrow of highborn, powerful figures such as kings. Miller, however, has argued that an ordinary person can serve equally well as tragic hero, if he wants something intensely enough to give up everything else in its pursuit. Actually, the "hero" need not be thoroughly clear as to his goals—Miller's tragic figures are often somewhat confused. Yet if there is something decent about what the hero seeks, he can still be regarded as making a truly tragic commitment.

For example, in *Death of a Salesman*, Willy Loman is confused about success and happiness and the obligations of parent and child. As a result, he gives his sons Biff and Happy unrealistic counsel about achieving happiness; and his eventual suicide to get the insurance money for Biff is a highly questionable solution to the family's problems. Yet Willy is a father who wants to provide well for his sons and leave them a splendid heritage. This is an admirable objective. According to the Miller theory, there is a recognizable tragic stature even in a poor, distracted, unimpressive salesman, if he is willing to give his life for his convictions.

Similar patterns are apparent in other Miller plays. Joe Keller in *All My Sons,* for example, puts the interests of his household above all else, letting the defective plane parts be shipped out from his factory rather than jeopardize the family business. When his son Chris rejects him, he can no longer see any reason to live and kills himself. In *A View from the Bridge*, longshoreman Eddie Carbone does not want his young niece to marry a light-hearted immigrant, Rodolpho. Eddie is jealous of the young man, which makes him hostile. Yet in his own way Eddie means well, and the drastic step he eventually takes to prevent the marriage costs him his own life.

In *The Crucible,* John Proctor is also a common man—a farmer—rather than a highborn leader. He is far from anxious to engage in any heroic action. In fact, he tends to be cautious, and even seriously considers confessing to a lie to save his life. But in the long run, he cannot sign a statement that he regards as false. So he goes to his death, his self-respect intact. Many critics who have hesitated about admitting the tragic stature of such muddled individuals as Willy and Eddie have been more than willing at least to concede it to sturdy, responsible John Proctor.

MILLER AND THE SOCIAL DRAMA

In addition to being classified as "psychological dramas" and "modern tragedies," Arthur Miller's works are sometimes listed as "social dramas." This last category refers to plays that deal with issues affecting contemporary society. Eugene O'Neill, John Steinbeck, and Clifford Odets were among the American playwrights before Miller who had taken up various social questions. Henrik Ibsen had done much to establish the genre many years before.

In *All My Sons*, Miller had considered the matter of public responsibility. Joe Keller is a reasonably good American family man who has even lost a son in the war. But Keller will send out defective products to the Army rather than lose contracts that may destroy his business. Like many of us, he wants to leave something valuable to his surviving son, Chris. But Chris—and obviously Miller—insists that as a man Keller has no right to destroy the sons of others to protect the material interests of his own. In developing this situation, Miller is clearly indicting all those Americans who take advantage of a national crisis to turn everything to their own selfish profit.

In *Death of a Salesman*, there are other aspects of American life that Miller views with suspicion. He objects to the callous, inhumane attitude of the business world, so competitive that it lacks consideration for workers as individuals. He also criticizes his countrymen's overemphasis upon material success, and their overstressing of superficial personality traits to the detriment of solid character building.

The Crucible again takes up the question of social responsibility. Obviously some people who support the witchcraft persecutions have strictly personal goals. Abigail wants revenge, Putnam wants more land, and the judges want to escape being accused of having acted unjustly. Yet all are shirking their responsibilities as human beings. When he considers the possibility of making a false confession, John

Proctor knows that in so doing he will betray his friends. Proctor, however, is a responsible man, and eventually does the right thing.

BIOGRAPHICAL SKETCH

Arthur Miller was born in New York City on October 17, 1915, the son of an Austrian-born clothing manufacturer. He grew up in Brooklyn, which he would use as the setting for *Death of a Salesman* and *A View from the Bridge*. In both plays he notes changes occurring during those years. Willy Loman, for instance, saw the almost rural area of small houses with flower and vegetable gardens yield to tall apartment buildings. Alfieri, the lawyer in the later work, saw its waterfront become more "civilized." Although Miller says little directly about his home life, there are at least autobiographical hints in his plays. The genial side of Joe Keller may well have been suggested by his father's good-natured joking and *After the Fall* indicates that his mother gave early encouragement to his literary promise.

After graduating from Brooklyn's Abraham Lincoln High School in 1932, Miller hoped to go to college, but the Depression had limited the family's finances. Several of his works reflect how hard men had to work to make a living during those years. Eddie, in *A View from the Bridge*, tells of the struggle to support his family and it is clear that both Joe Keller and Willy Loman never found it very easy to forge ahead. In any event, to earn money toward a higher education, young Miller worked for two years in a warehouse supplying automobile parts. Then he was able to go on to the University of Michigan. There he won the Avery Hopwood Award for his first play, *The Grass Still Grows*. He went on then to write other dramas, completing his college course by means of a part-time newspaper job and help from the National Youth Administration.

Returning east after his 1938 graduation, Miller continued to write plays while holding various posts to make a living. He worked in a box factory and the Navy Yard, drove a truck, waited on tables, and served as crewman on a tanker. He also was connected with the Federal Theatre Project, wrote radio scripts, and did research for a film. In 1944 he brought out a war commentary, *Situation Normal,* and in the following year he published a novel against anti-Semitism, called *Focus. The Man Who Had All the Luck* was his first Broadway play, produced in 1944. But he did not win success until *All My Sons* was produced three years later and *Death of a Salesman* in 1949.

Both *All My Sons* and *Death of a Salesman* deal with the business and domestic problems of middle-class American families. Both concern a father in conflict with two sons whose love and respect he ardently desires. In *All My Sons,* Joe Keller wants to leave his boys a thriving business. But one, Larry, dies in the war. The other, Chris, is appalled to learn that while he was fighting overseas, his father shipped out defective plane parts. Rejected and condemned by his surviving son, Keller commits suicide. Never so prosperous as Joe Keller, Willy Loman in *Death of a Salesman* also has great hopes for his sons, especially the elder, Biff. Willy brags to both sons that he is well-liked, and assures them a great future awaits. Biff, disillusioned when he discovers his father's sexual deceptions, drifts from job to job, while Happy resentfully makes up for his insignificant position by sensual self-indulgence. Unable to accept their failure and his own, Willy kills himself so that he can at least leave Biff some insurance money.

In 1953 Miller offered *The Crucible,* a drama based upon the 1690s Massachusetts witchcraft trials. In our own time, the term "witch hunt" was sometimes used to describe various investigations launched by Congressional and other groups to expose un-American activities. Since it was understood that Miller himself had little sympathy for such official inquiries, many sought to reduce his play to simple allegory. Actually it is no mere propaganda piece, although certainly there is, by implication, criticism of the attitudes and methods of some later interrogators. Subsequently Miller himself was to be called before a congressional committee and convicted for failing to cite the names of those formerly known to have engaged in radical activities.

The Crucible tells of the havoc wrought in early Salem when some restless young girls claim that witches are taking over the village. Their leader, the beautiful and vindictive Abigail Williams, hopes for revenge against Elizabeth Proctor, from whose service she was dismissed after having had an affair with Elizabeth's husband, John. As more accusations are made, and many, including Elizabeth, arrested, John Proctor joins with other sensible townsmen to stop the outrages. Charged himself and imprisoned, he must decide whether to live by swearing to a vicious lie, or going to his death rather than denying the truth. He makes the second choice.

In September, 1955, Miller offered a double bill of two short works, neither of which was particularly well received. The first, *A Memory of Two Mondays,* was a brief mood piece, based upon his youthful experiences in the auto-parts ware-house. The young office boy, Bert, who takes the job, as did Miller, to earn money for college, manifests a friendly interest in the joys and sorrows of fellow employees, while wonder-ing how they go on seemingly content with routine work over the years. When he leaves, however, he is saddened to realize how readily they will forget him. Snatches of poetry and certain softening effects in set and lighting cast an almost romantic glow over mundane happenings in the drab, dingy old factory.

In *A View from the Bridge*, Miller described Brooklyn residents very different culturally from those in *Death of a Salesman*. Again, however, the tone was tragic, and conflict was developed between family members of two generations. Again the father figure would seek blindly to safeguard the future for the young, and again be rejected and go to his death violently. Eddie Carbone, a hard-working longshoreman, is overly fond of his wife's niece, Catherine. When the girl falls in love with Rodolpho, an illegal immigrant sheltered by the Carbone family, Eddie convinces himself that the marriage would not be a good one for Catherine. Unable to dissuade her, he eventually turns informer and dies in a knife duel with Rodolpho's irate brother. He is another unyielding Miller hero, willing to give up everything for his tenaciously held belief. Dissatisfied with the work's original form, Miller later expanded the piece to a full-length play. Revived off-Broadway during the 1964–1965 season, this longer form was now hailed with enthusiasm as a strong, effective tragic drama.

In 1956 and 1957, Miller was summoned before congressional committees and found guilty of contempt of Congress. This conviction was later reversed. Also during this period were marital difficulties. After a divorce from his first wife, Mary Slattery, by whom he had two children, in 1956, Miller married the well-known motion-picture star Marilyn Monroe. With her in mind, he wrote a poignant story, *The Misfits*, and adapted it for the screen. She starred in the film with Clark Gable. But this union, too, ended in divorce, and he subsequently wed a young European woman, Ingeborg Morath.

After the Fall opened at the new American National Theatre and Academy (ANTA) theater in New York in 1964. Like *Death of a Salesman, After the Fall* uses flashbacks to show what memories affect a man's thinking, but here all action takes place in the head of its hero, the lawyer, Quentin. The setting is colorless and almost abstract and characters appear and vanish readily as Quentin thinks about them. Twice divorced and considering a third marriage to a German girl, Quentin reviews his life to date. He recalls unhappy scenes with his first wife, Louise. He painfully relives episodes occurring at the time old friends were summoned before congressional committees. And above all, he keeps referring to his turbulent second marriage to an unstable blonde entertainer, Maggie, who later died a suicide. He finally takes heart from the counsels of Holga, the German girl, to accept his limitations and go on with courage and hope. The autobiographical element in this work attracted considerable attention. In particular, the rather sensational scenes with Maggie, the self-deceiving singer lost through drink and drugs, gave rise to comment. The format was also the subject of controversy, some finding it too diffuse for any satisfactory development of plot or characters.

Incident in Vichy was produced the same year. This somewhat shorter work deals more fully with the question of Nazi crimes raised in *After the Fall*. In 1942, ten men, suspected of being Jewish, are brought in for questioning in Vichy, France. As the play proceeds, the ten prisoners speculate fearfully as to their fate, hopefully exploring every suggestion that all may yet be well. Audiences in general seem to find this work a moving experience. The stakes are high, the suspense is continual, and the discussions are lively and revealing.

Arthur Miller continues to be considered one of the most important American playwrights. Most anthologies and histories of the drama in this country give space to his works, and his plays are staged around the world. Of course, he has not escaped adverse criticism. His language has been called banal and lacking in emotional power. He has been attacked as too negative in his view of American society and especially as being unfair to American business. Again there have been those who have rejected his concept of tragedy as meanly bourgeois, regarding his "common man" heroes as "little" and "common" in the worst sense, or not genuinely human enough to qualify as tragic figures at all. Nor have his technical approaches been universally approved. The Act One "Overture" to *The Crucible* has annoyed some commentators, and the terminal "Requiem" to *Death of a Salesman* has annoyed others.

Yet the very prevalence of so much controversy over this dramatist testifies to his influential position in the American theater. Regardless of objections posed to this or that individual aspect of his work, he retains an essentially unchallenged reputation. And even those who take issue with him admire his continuing efforts to devise suitable new forms to express new and different themes. Even among those who disagree with his literary, political, and social views, there are many who still find him a stimulating writer, one who at least does do some thinking about vital contemporary issues. Finally, audiences for two decades have found his plays good theater. They have wept over the death of poor, battered old Willy Loman, and have been awed by the plain-spoken, solid integrity of John Proctor. They have watched fascinated as deluded Eddie baits Rodolpho, they have listened with shock to the tirades of the embittered Maggie, and they have sympathized warmly with the diffidently heroic Austrian prince. Whatever else may be said, Miller commands the attention and stirs the hearts of most who come to see his dramas. This gift is what most conclusively labels him a major playwright.

DEATH OF A SALESMAN
CHARACTERS

WILLY LOMAN
The salesman, over sixty, beaten and exhausted, who once dreamed that he and his sons would achieve success by being well-liked.

LINDA
His devoted and patient wife, who would have Willy's sons treat him with compassion and respect.

BIFF
Their older son, thirty-four, ruggedly built but disheartened, partial to outdoor farm work but afraid that it offers no future.

HAPPY
His brother, thirty-two, a slick, dapper clerk. He accepts bribes and brags about his sensual affairs, but he talks of settling down with a good wife like Mom.

BERNARD
The slight, studious boy next door, who grows up to be a flourishing young lawyer.

CHARLEY
Bernard's father, an unassuming, quietly plodding business-man, who proves a loyal friend to Willy, "lending" him hundreds of dollars to salvage his self-respect.

UNCLE BEN
Willy's almost legendary older brother, whose talk of dazzling fortunes made quickly in Alaska and Africa filled Willy with tantalizing visions.

HOWARD WAGNER
Old Man Wagner's shallow, unresponsive son.

JENNY

Charley's secretary. She is little afraid of Willy when he seems overwrought and confused.

OLD MAN WAGNER

Willy's original boss. He thought highly of Willy and predicted that Willy would eventually become a partner in the firm.

STANLEY

An accommodating waiter at Frank's Chop House. He is suitably impressed with Happy's bravado air of being a connoisseur of rare wines and beautiful women.

MISS FORSYTHE

An elegant, attractive young prostitute whom Happy suavely picks up in the restaurant.

LETTA

The woman who Miss Forsythe obligingly provides for Biff, at Happy's request. She is an outgoing type and looks forward to jury duty.

THE WOMAN

A Boston buyer, whose casual affair with Willy did much to shatter young Biff's shining image of his father.

DEATH OF A SALESMAN
SETTING

Much of the "action" really occurs inside Willy's disturbed mind, as he relives crucial scenes from the past even while groping through present-day encounters. The rest of the action takes place in the kitchen and two bedrooms of Willy's modest Brooklyn house. The home was once practically suburban but is now crowded in by high apartment buildings. Other locations, such as Howard's office, the restaurant, and the Boston hotel room, are set up on the stage apron with clever lighting and a few basic props. (The lighting involves the projection of a pattern of leaves on the stage during Willy's mental retreats from the present into the past, the density of the leaves indicating the extent of his withdrawal from reality, and the leaves themselves providing a symbolic reference to the more rural circumstances of the past.) Haunting flute music is used on occasion to set the mood.

DEATH OF A SALESMAN
PLOT SUMMARY

ACT I

Wearily hauling in his big sample cases, Willy Loman, a salesman over sixty years old, returns unexpectedly to his Brooklyn home. On the way to appointments in New England, he tells his worried wife, Linda, he kept losing control of his car and had to come back home. Linda urges him to ask Howard Wagner, his young boss, for easier work in town. She also tries cheering him with the news that their grown sons, Biff and Happy, are together again upstairs, amicably sharing their old room.

Willy is concerned about Biff, thirty-four, who has just quit one more farm job out West. How can such an impressive lad be so lost, Willy wonders. Willy also regrets that their house, at last almost paid for, has been gradually hemmed in by soaring apartments. He misses the earlier country scents of spring flowers.

Upstairs, the boys, roused by Willy's arrival, laughingly recall their first flings with women. Biff, troubled, admits smarting under Willy's disapproval but says he found the routine of office and sales work too confining. He likes herding cattle better but fears that it offers no future. Happy, younger and cockier, can afford an apartment, a car, and the sexual affairs he craves. But Happy envies the highly paid merchandise manager, and so gets even with him by taking bribes and seducing the fiancées of fellow employees. He would, however, like to settle down with a good girl like his mother. He is tempted by Biff's invitation to join him in some outdoor ranch project, but first wants to equal the manager as regards salary and prestige. Biff, in turn, talks of floating a loan from Bill Oliver, a sporting-goods man, whose employ he abruptly quit long ago after stealing a carton of basketballs.

Meanwhile, Willy sits alone in the kitchen eating a snack. He relives a cherished memory. Biff and Happy are in high school age. One afternoon, they have proudly and energetically shined up the family car. Much pleased, Willy gives them a punching bag and is undismayed to learn that Biff has stolen a football from school. Willy's sons idolize him, and he boasts of his sales prowess. Young Bernard, the studious boy next door, warns that Biff is failing math and may not graduate. Willy scoffs at this, citing athletic-scholarship prospects. He predicts greater success for his sons since they are better liked than the conscientious Bernard.

A younger Linda enters with the wash. Having bragged to her of big sales, he quickly cuts his estimate when he learns how much they need for car payments and household repairs. He adds that he is not so sure of himself as he pretends. When Linda reassures him, his mind reverts guiltily to compliments paid him by a Boston buyer with whom he had an affair. He also is disturbed by new reports of Biff's wildness.

Willy's mind comes back to the present. Charley, Bernard's father, comes over to soothe Willy with a card game. Willy, however, remains nervous and irritable. Something Charley says makes him recall his older brother, Ben, and Willy flashes back to the past.

Willy remembers a brief visit when Ben told him about making a fortune quickly in African diamonds. Ben also recounted how their father crossed the country with them in a wagon selling flutes. Ben urges Willy to try his fortune in Alaska and gives young Biff a lesson in fighting ruthlessly, jungle style. Charley warns that Biff is taking lumber from building projects, but Willy sees this as initiative. He sneers at Charley and Bernard as unable even to hammer nails.

Again in the present, Linda and the boys try to get Willy to bed, but he insists upon taking a walk, even though he is

wearing slippers rather than shoes. Linda rebukes Biff for stay-
ing away and then quarreling with Willy. She loves her
husband deeply, and feels that even if he is collapsing now
he deserves respect as a person. After more than thirty years,
Willy's employer has taken him off salary and put him back
on straight commission. The boys are shocked by this news
and are saddened even more to hear that Willy has been
attempting to kill himself. Once he drove his car off the road,
and he keeps some tubing handy for inhaling gas. Biff promises reform, but upon Willy's return they once again argue
bitterly. Willy, however, is delighted to hear of Biff's plan to
approach Oliver. Willy tells Biff to request a large sum of
money and act as if he were already prosperous. Biff and
Happy talk further of organizing teams to sell a line of sports
equipment. Despite some further bickering, all are buoyed up
with hope: Happy says he will get married, Willy will see
Howard, and even the moon shines brightly on the little house.

ACT II

The next morning, Willy, well rested and confident, prepares
to face Howard. The boys have already left, with Biff looking
handsome and assured. Linda reminds Willy that they need
about two hundred dollars to cover the insurance premium,
repairs, and the last home mortgage payment. The house will
finally be all theirs, and Willy proudly recalls the good
carpentering he did to make it strong and safe. Linda also
gives him the welcome word that his boys will take him to
dinner that night.

At the office Willy can hardly get Howard's attention because
the boss is more interested in his latest toy, a costly new tape
recorder. Finally made to listen, Howard disclaims a Christmas party pledge to find Willy a New York job, and remains
unyielding as the salesman desperately offers to work for less
and less money. Angered, Willy recalls an earlier business
world in which selling aroused respect and gratitude. Then
old Dave Singleman, eighty-four, in green velvet slippers, could

sit in his hotel room anywhere and sell buyers by phone. Howard will not hear of old promises made to Willy by his father, and eventually fires Willy, despite Willy's eagerness to try the Boston route again.

Again reverting to the past, Willy recalls Ben urging him to seek his fortune in Alaska. Then, however, Linda had stressed the good prospects in his sales job. Willy then relives the day of Biff's last football triumph at Ebbets Field. Even Bernard pleads to carry the shoulder guards, but Charley chides Willy, half-jokingly, for letting a game mean so much at his age.

Back in the present, Willy makes a distractedly noisy entrance into Charley's office, upsetting Jenny, his secretary. There with luggage and tennis rackets is Bernard, now a pleasant, confident young lawyer. He is off to try a case before the Supreme Court. After pitiably bluffing about Biff's prosperity, Willy sadly asks Bernard why Biff gave up. Puzzled himself, Bernard admits that Biff really lost heart not after the math failure but after a trip to Boston to meet Willy. This information disturbs Willy further.

Willy then asks for and receives a large sum from Charley but refuses the latter's well-meant offer of a job. His benefactor disputes the idea that success stems from being well liked, and also sharply denies that Willy would be worth more dead. As he leaves, Willy sobs that Charley is his one friend.

At Frank's Chop House, Happy impresses the waiter, Stanley, with his sophisticated airs and deftly picks up an attractive prostitute, Miss Forsythe. Then he sends her for a friend for Biff. He tells Miss Forsythe that Biff is rich and famous.

Biff arrives and glumly admits that Oliver had no time for his former shipping clerk. Impulsively, Biff stole his fountain pen, but he knows now that his life has been one great lie. Willy joins them, in no mood to have Biff facing hard facts. Drifting again back into the past, he relives the distressing scene in which the idolizing Biff caught him in a hotel room with the lady buyer. Biff had angrily denounced his father as a lying fake and dropped plans for going to college.

In the present, coming back to the table after a trip to the men's room, Willy is dismayed to find boys and prostitutes gone. Hurt, he tips Stanley well and goes off, oddly, to buy seeds. Later, Happy and Biff return home with flowers for Linda. She is furious and orders both to leave home and stop tormenting their father. Willy is in the garden, planting the seeds. Willy discusses with the phantom of Ben the merits of killing himself and leaving the twenty thousand dollars in insurance for Biff. It would be a great gesture, and he would have a huge funeral. Ready to leave, Biff argues that Willy should never have filled him or himself with such blown-up ideas of their own importance. Biff admits that he has been in jail for stealing a suit. They quarrel further, but Biff breaks down. Willy, convinced at last of his son's love, knows what he must do. Over Linda's fearful protests, he drives off in his car to kill himself.

REQUIEM

Charley, Bernard, and the three Lomans are the only mourners at Willy's funeral. Linda grieves that he had to die just when the house was finally theirs. They talk of Willy's fine carpentering, and Charley envisions him as riding on "a smile and a shoeshine." Biff decides to head west again, but Happy still wants to make Willy's grandiose ideas work. Alone, Linda sobbingly asks why Willy killed himself. They had their house and could now at last have been really free.

DEATH OF A SALESMAN
ANALYSIS: ACT I

ACT I, SCENE 1

Willy Loman, an aging Brooklyn salesman, returns home exhausted and irritable late one Monday night. His loyal wife, Linda, is alarmed, for by now he should be in New England on a sales trip. He tells her, however, that he could not concentrate and kept driving his car off the road. She suggests that rest might help and urges him to seek office work near home. Their grown sons, Biff and Happy, amiably reunited, are asleep upstairs. Biff, thirty-four, has just come back from one more temporary farm job. Angered and concerned, Willy cannot see how so promising a youth can be so lost. He also regrets peevishly that their house, now almost paid for, has lost its country surroundings of grass and flowers and is now hemmed in by tall apartments. He muses about the happier past, back in 1928, when the smiling, popular young Biff used to polish so expertly their old red Chevrolet.

CHARACTER ANALYSES

This opening scene introduces significant aspects of Willy's personality. A few of Linda's traits also are revealed, and there are brief descriptive references to the still unseen Biff, Happy, and Willy's young boss, Howard.

WILLY

Willy appears first as a tired, worn man of sixty. His weariness is apparent in the hunched-over, stooped way in which he carries in his heavy sample cases. Besides, he himself says that he is weary, and Linda insists more than once that he needs rest and a less demanding job assignment.

He is also obviously shaken. His work as a salesman requires him to do a great deal of driving, and now he seems unable to keep his car under control. He rejects Linda's comforting assurance that he may have some easily solved problem, such as needing new glasses. He is especially frightened when he realizes that although he was behind the wheel of his current Studebaker, he actually thought for a time that he was still steering the old red Chevrolet he owned in 1928.

Thirdly, he is short-tempered. He answers Linda sharply, retorts angrily when accused of criticizing Biff, and is unreasonably irked to be offered whipped cheese instead of his customary Swiss. He testily complains about the unopened windows and condemns the builders of apartment houses for ruining the neighborhood.

In addition, he is worried, especially about Biff. Why has he not found himself some steady work and settled down? Is it mere laziness? Willy wants him to make a good living and is at a loss to understand why he cannot. This combination of anxiety and bewilderment has led Willy to greet his returning son with reproachful questions, and relations are strained between them. Willy also hopes that he is not causing Linda to fret, for she is his source of strength.

Finally, Willy reveals the wistfulness of a dreamer. This is emphasized subtly by the plaintive, light theme played on the flute as background music. Moreover, there is his delighted response to the pleasant scenery along the road, as well as his recollections of the lilac, wisteria, and peonies that used to give out a springtime fragrance before the apartment builders "massacred" the neighborhood. There is nostalgia, too, as he thinks of the smiling, popular younger Biff, who shined up the Chevrolet so beautifully that no one would believe it had gone eighty thousand miles.

LINDA

Linda is shown here to be patient, tactful, and considerate. Even when the tired, peevish Willy is rude, she keeps her temper and tries to soothe him. Lovingly she takes off his shoes and makes every effort to restore his confidence in himself.

Yet she is clearly no mere passive wife. She takes issue with Willy for talking so harshly to Biff and tells him to control himself. She would have him do nothing to dishearten further this troubled young man who is still trying to find himself. She also ventures to cut in on his tirade against the apartment builders with the remark that others have to live somewhere. Moreover, she is quite insistent that he see Howard about a less taxing position.

Although Linda, in general, murmurs reassuring words to Willy, she is shown from the first to possess a realistic awareness of the true situation. Her remark that Willy's "mind is overactive" is shrewdly perceptive, and she shows a sensitive appreciation of Biff's discouragement and confusion.

BIFF

Although only discussed here, Biff is represented as a cheerful, eager, well-liked boy who for some reason grew up to be a moody, restless young man. For over ten years now, he has gone from job to job and never made much money. That he still has some pride is hinted when Linda dodges the question of his apologizing to Willy. But that he is also sensitive is suggested by her statement that he was "crestfallen" after Willy criticized him. Her comment here also indicates that Biff admires his father and cares a great deal about the older man's opinion of him.

The question of Biff's laziness is left open. Willy seems undecided, and he recalls the boy Biff as energetically simonizing the car. Linda, on her part, denies that he is lazy. She describes him as "lost," but offers no helpful explanation as to how their son lost his earlier breezy confidence.

HAPPY

Virtually nothing is said of the younger son, Happy. He is clearly not on Willy's mind now and does not figure prominently in Willy's recollections, as shown up to now. He is merely said to get along well with his brother and to have taken him out with him on a date. Later it will be evident that Happy is a sensual young man, much given to casual love affairs. Here he is placed in the general family picture, but not accorded much importance.

HOWARD

Willy's young boss is the son of "old man Wagner," who held great hopes out to Willy and treated him well. With the encouragement of that masterly prince, Willy opened up the New England territory for the firm. The son, however, shows little appreciation, and this implied coldness will crucially affect Willy's life later in the play.

PLOT DEVELOPMENT

WILLY AND HIS JOB

Willy's difficulties with the car suggest that his job may be in jeopardy. Linda, for all her reassuring manner, suggests that as he is over sixty he cannot be expected to do so much traveling. At her urging, he agrees to go ask Howard for a New York assignment. But the references to Howard's unappreciative nature indicate that Willy may meet opposition.

WILLY AND BIFF

It is evident that relations are tense and uneasy between father and son. Remembering the smiling lively youngster Biff used to be, Willy is disgusted with the thirty-four-year-old moody drifter. Yet he does want to help Biff, so he promises Linda to hold his temper, and try to find the youth a selling job. If, however, Biff prefers to return West, he will let him go without rancor. But Willy is seen to be so irritable and impulsive that further hostilities seem likely.

TECHNIQUE

In later scenes Willy's mind will slip back to past scenes, and he will be seen talking to such memory characters as the young boy Biff or the now dead Uncle Ben. You might find such flashbacks confusing in the opening scene, when you meet the characters for the first time. Here, Willy does drift back to earlier days. He thinks of his first years with the company, Biff's popularity as a boy, the former flower gardens around the house, and the 1928 car polishing. These recollections, however, are conveyed only through Willy's dialogue, with the music of the flute sometimes adding a touch of strangeness. In general, then, this first episode takes place clearly in the present and makes virtually no use of the interesting stage devices later employed to show memories being reenacted in Willy's disturbed consciousness.

IMPORTANT THEMES

"LOSTNESS"

Willy says that for an instant while driving he could not remember the last few minutes. Again, he thought he was in the old Chevrolet instead of the current Studebaker. Willy is literally as well as symbolically lost. At sixty, moreover, he is clearly unsure of himself, worried about his job and about his son. If Biff, who cannot seem to find a satisfying way of life at thirty-four, is "lost," so, in another way, is his sixty-year-old father.

FATHER-SON CONFLICT

Willy cannot accept Linda's idea that life is a "casting off." Biff is no longer a small boy; he is a grown man thirty-four years old. Yet Willy still angrily criticizes Biff failing to succeed. He cannot stop thinking about Biff's problems and says that he will try to get him a job. According to Linda, Biff is badly upset when his father criticizes him, but still keeps coming home, unwilling to make a break. These two men are thus extremely concerned about each other, but from the first there are also deep hostilities that will lead to more and more violent arguments.

CHANGED LIVING CONDITIONS
When the younger Willy and Linda first started making payments on their Brooklyn house, it was in a pleasant semi-rural area with grass and flower and vegetable gardens. Since then, however, tall apartment houses have been built that shut out the light so that plants will not grow. There are now unpleasant odors in place of the fragrance of lilac and wisteria. Willy's little house and the hammock he and Biff swung between the elms thus becomes the symbol of an earlier, more individualistic, more easy-going America. The big apartments in turn suggest to Willy a population "out of control" and the new "maddening" competition. Only a few buildings in a small area are involved here, but the playwright seems to suggest that the changes may be typical in America.

CHANGED BUSINESS CONDITIONS
When Willy began selling for the Wagner company, he opened up whole new territories and was properly commended by his employer, a "prince," who was "masterful." Now, however, the business is under the direction of Howard, the old employer's son. Howard is not one to appreciate long, loyal service. This theme will be developed further as the play proceeds. The cold, impersonal tone of business today will be contrasted with the friendlier, more humane spirit of past transactions.

LAMENT FOR THE PAST
The tone of the play is often nostalgic. In this scene, Willy looks back to better times when old Wagner was his boss and his house had a flourishing garden. He recalls how well-liked Biff was as a boy and how beautiful the red Chevrolet looked when polished. The present, by contrast, is a time of darkness and suffocation, of weariness and bewilderment, of blighted hopes and bitter quarrels.

ACT I, SCENE 2

Upstairs in their old bedroom, the two sons are roused by Willy's noisy mumbling. Both are worried about him but none-theless they are soon cheerfully reminiscing about their early affairs with prostitutes. Biff is ill at ease, however, aware of his father's scorn. He also feels that he should have settled down, but he has hated the routine and competition of steady jobs, and the more pleasant ranch work he has found finan-cially unprofitable. Happy, in turn, has his own apartment, car, and feminine conquests. But he, too, longs for outdoor muscular work. Biff envisions a ranch they could handle together, but Happy still first wants the prestige of a large income. Biff thinks he might obtain a loan from Bill Oliver, an early employer, whom he left after stealing some basketballs. They hear Willy again, and Biff denounces him angrily.

CHARACTER ANALYSES

This scene concerns the two Loman brothers almost exclu-sively. Only brief references are made to Willy and Linda.

WILLY

Heard by the boys to mumble about the mileage on the old Chevrolet and Biff's expert car polishing, Willy unnerves Happy and infuriates Biff. The sons' comments point up the fact that Willy's odd behavior has been going on for some time and is getting worse. Recently, Happy sent his father to Florida for a rest cure, but to no avail. Happy confirms the impression created in Scene 1 that Willy is mainly upset about Biff's drift-ing from job to job.

LINDA

To Happy, Linda represents the type of admirable woman he would willingly marry, as contrasted with the girls of easy virtue with whom he regularly has affairs. His mother has high standards and is incorruptible. To Biff, however, Linda appears the victim of Willy's boorish, inconsiderate actions. He is incensed that she should have to listen to his father's wild outbursts.

BIFF

In Scene 2, Biff is antagonistic toward his father, protectively concerned about Linda, comradely toward Happy, and confused and anxious as to his own future. At first Biff is reticent about his attitude toward Willy, although referring to him with no enthusiasm. Then, looking glum, he asks Happy why his father always seems to view him mockingly. However, he angrily rejects his brother's suggestion that he is the cause of Willy's erratic mumbling. Later when the latter's wild talk becomes more audible, Biff reacts with fury and contempt. His father seems a self-centered, doltish man who disrupts the family. Still, Biff appears momentarily grief-stricken when he hears Willy refer to the old car-polishing days. There is pain as well as anger in Biff's "sour" rejection of Willy.

His references to Linda are few, but she is clearly someone he loves and admires. Although it is Happy who says he would like to find a girl like his mother, Biff also wants one who is "steady" and has "substance." It is quite possible that he, too, sees her as an ideal type. Certainly, he is furious that she should be subjected to Willy's noisy, rambling talk. Later it will become evident why Biff's grudge against Willy has made him especially sorry for his mother.

Biff seems to be genuinely fond of his younger brother. He amusedly recalls the time years ago when he first took Happy out with him on dates with prostitutes. He dreams of taking Happy out West so they can run a ranch together. He could trust Happy and they could both enjoy the outdoor work.

In general, Biff seems to Happy to have lost his good spirits and self-confidence. For one thing, Biff is dissatisfied with his life. For years now he has gone from one temporary job to the next, and he feels this is the irresponsible way of a boy, not a grown man. He believes that he should marry some good, steady girl and settle down in some line of work. In this view he is thus in substantial agreement with Willy.

Yet he is uncertain which way to turn. He has held various business jobs and found them suffocating. He hated the routine, the indoor confinement, and the strong competitive spirit. Yet he realizes that such work pays well and makes it possible for a young man to become established. On the other hand, he has found considerable satisfaction in the open-air ranch work he has done in the West. For instance, he likes to see the young colts in the spring. But the pay is low, and the future is not promising.

His solution at the moment is to try to obtain a loan and buy a ranch. This way he could do the type of work he likes and still have some stability. He plans to approach a former employer, Bill Oliver, for the loan. Here his thinking seems somewhat fuzzy. He quit Oliver's company shortly after stealing a carton of basketballs, and he thinks that Oliver suspected the truth. It is thus not at all clear why Oliver should lend such a dubious risk several thousand dollars. In terms of Biff's mentality, however, the move is curiously plausible. Oliver, who once used to trust Biff, did tell him to ask him if he ever needed anything. This may well have been merely a conventional form of polite farewell, but Willy and Biff place much emphasis upon the personal bond in business. Despite all evidence to the contrary, their concept of economic relationships seems constantly to stress a man-to-man, informal, friendly meeting of individuals. Willy will talk to Howard, and all will be well. Biff will go back to the businessman who a decade or so ago put a reassuring hand on his shoulder, and will walk out with a ten-thousand-dollar loan.

Two other factors enter into Biff's vision of Oliver, which identify Biff again as truly Willy's son. One is a streak of buoyant optimism that is hard to erase. Charley, a neighbor, will later eulogize Willy as a salesman "riding on a smile and a shoeshine." At this time in their lives both Willy and Biff are unhappy and discouraged, yet every so often each suddenly feels an upsurge of confidence. Here, even to think of floating such a large loan from his ex-employer, Biff must have some of this hopeful enthusiasm.

Ironically, there is also an underlying sense of desperation. Like his father, Biff is beaten. He does not know what to do or where to turn, so he will seize upon almost any possibility. Only a man brought up to "think big" and concoct grandiose schemes could dream up the Oliver loan project. But Biff, who actually does voice some misgivings, has no other prospects at all. As a result, he will have to convince himself that Oliver did at least formerly think the world of him and may still be willing to hand him a sizable sum.

HAPPY

Like his father and Biff, Happy is described as a strong, muscular, athletic type. He holds a reasonably well-paying job in a store, but he does not find the work itself satisfying. Like his brother, he would rather use his muscles and take on more strenuous activities in the open air. Yet he is not likely to accept Biff's invitation to join him out West.

Never Willy's favorite, Happy wants the respect and prestige that a lucrative job will guarantee. When the high-salaried merchandise manager enters the store, "waves part in front of him." Those who give Happy orders at work are not only "common" and "petty," but "pompous" and "self-important." Happy is determined to show them that he, too, can achieve success on their terms.

Happy wants what his bosses possess, all the while regarding them with contempt. His confidence is based on three factors. First, Willy always suggested that his sons were destined for greatness. As Biff says in this scene, they were not brought up to "grub for money." Secondly, Happy is very conscious of his physical strength and prowess. He thus resents being ordered around by those who cannot box so well, run so fast, or lift such heavy weights. Thirdly, he is proud of the fact that women find him attractive. He has even been able to seduce the fiancées of three store executives. In his view, he must be more virile and impressive than they are.

At the same time, he recognizes certain other deplorable aspects of his present way of life. For one thing, he is aware that material wealth does not in itself assure contentment. The merchandise manager, whom he envies, built an impressive house on Long Island, only to move out and start another within a few months. And even Happy, who can at least boast of his own apartment, his own car, and a steady supply of admiring women, admits he is often lonely and dissatisfied.

In addition, he does not like the intensely competitive spirit. If he were with someone like Biff, whom he could trust, he might be able to live up to his ideals. He would presumably be honest and would not tempt the fiancées of other men. Instead he would settle down with a good, dependable girl like his mother. Since he claims that everyone around him is corrupt, he takes bribes from buyers, ruins the future wives of his bosses, and eyes his fellow workers with smoldering hostility.

A sensual man, he apparently has many casual love affairs. He gets some pleasure from these dubious romances. In addition, they help provide temporary escape from loneliness and frustration. They make him feel popular and important and—especially when the girls are the other men's fiancées—more attractive than business rivals. Yet he must admit that often there is little thrill obtained from such brief relationships. He feels vaguely guilty about his continual self-indulgence, so he tells Biff that what he really wants is marriage with a nice, respectable girl. Yet in order to change, he would, of course, have to give up the affairs. While these have not given him the deeper rewards of a permanent relationship, they have helped to serve as some compensation for his decidedly subordinate position at work. They act as props for Happy's ego; and despite his repeated assurances of imminent reform, he will not readily do without these minor triumphs.

Happy is not altogether ungenerous. He seems to have financed Willy's brief and unavailing Florida rest cure. He is concerned for his father's worsening condition. Yet he was never the favored son, and he is not so emotionally shattered by the situation as is Biff. He asks Biff's help because Willy's behavior is "getting embarrassing." Biff is more likely to think of his mother's sufferings, but Happy, in general, is used to looking out mainly for himself.

PLOT DEVELOPMENT

Most of this scene is taken up with exposition regarding the personalities and histories of the two sons. The only important plot element introduced here is Biff's plan to ask Oliver for a loan. This scheme will eventually have a crucial bearing upon relations between Biff and his father and will help bring about Willy's last momentous decision.

TECHNIQUE

This scene is essentially dialogue. During the boys' conversation, Willy can be heard apparently addressing the boy Biff who long ago so expertly simonized the car. The scene functions to introduce two more main characters, and there is little evidence of any unusual or startling stage devices. Having a set that shows more than one room makes it possible to show Willy muttering in the kitchen while the boys talk upstairs. But the time sequence is chronological and events occur objectively, not solely in Willy's mind.

IMPORTANT THEMES

LOSTNESS

Neither Biff nor Happy is contented. At thirty-four, Biff has no job and only the most doubtful of prospects (the Oliver plan). The outdoor work he likes offers no security and no future.

The steady jobs that pay well have never held his interest long. He does not know what to do next. Happy is better established. He has a fair position, a car, and an apartment, but he feels that all is false around him and that he is constantly going back on his principles. Beneath his air of jaunty assurance, he, too, is anxious and confused.

FATHER-SON CONFLICT

Biff is both annoyed and concerned about Willy. Hearing Willy's noisy mumbling, he becomes furious at his father for disturbing his mother. Happy is also worried about Willy but is annoyed because the older man's erratic behavior is "embarrassing."

CORRUPTION IN MODERN BUSINESS

Well-built men, Biff and Happy prefer working with their muscles in the outdoors. Both object to the confinement and routine of store or office work. Such attitudes may be merely matters of individual temperament, rather than indications of some flaw in the overall system. Yet throughout the play there is some suggestion that the wilder, freer life of those who earlier pushed Westward offered greater satisfactions to the strong individual who was good with his hands. In the indoor world, according to the resentful Happy, meaner, commoner types give orders to those whose physical prowess they could not hope to match.

Both Biff and Happy also criticize the intensely competitive spirit of business. Biff can not see why he must always try to get ahead of the next man. Happy feels that this sense of competition drives him to seduce the fiancées of store executives. Yet while he deplores this emphasis, noting that getting ahead does not guarantee bliss, he still wants to prove his worth by making more money than the merchandise manager. The brothers wish they could be business partners. Each then would have someone to trust, and they would presumably be working with, not against each other.

Taken as a whole, the views expressed by Biff and Happy are not, of course, necessarily those of the playwright. These two young men have rather obvious personality flaws. Neither is a mature, sensible, truly adult individual. When, for instance, Happy sneers at his fellow employees, he is probably revealing more about his own faults than about theirs. Yet there is sufficient stress upon the coldly competitive spirit in the business world, here and elsewhere in the play, to suggest that this may be Miller's observation.

COUNTRY VERSUS CITY

Nineteenth-century Romantic poets such as William Wordsworth wrote that those who lived in the country, close to Nature and its wonders, were likely to be happier, nobler people than those forced to endure the ugliness of crowded cities. Here Biff's lyrical talks of the Western farm in the spring, with fifteen fine new colts, contrasts with Happy's disgruntled account of the competition, bribery, and questionable love affairs that characterize his urban world. Willy remembers the more rural Brooklyn of sweet-smelling flower gardens and feels stifled in the new city atmosphere of tall apartments with more and more people.

ACT I, SCENE 3
SUMMARY

Willy urges young Biff to finish his education before taking any girl seriously. But Biff's popularity pleases him. Willy is joined on stage by his sons in high-school garb, and he praises both lads for their work on the car. Just back from a trip, Willy surprises them with a new punching bag. Biff, in turn, displays a new football, stolen from the locker room. Willy, laughing, commends his daring. Willy brags that he will some day own his own business, bigger than that of their neighbor, Charley, who is less "well liked." He tells of greeting the Mayor of Providence and promises the boys a summer ride through New England with him. The big football game is set for Saturday, and Biff pledges a special touchdown for Willy.

CHARACTER ANALYSES

This scene reveals more of the personalities of Willy and Biff, with some brief glimpses of the younger Happy.

WILLY

The episode which Willy now relives occurred some fifteen years before. The fact that it is now uppermost in the salesman's troubled mind indicates the kind of life experiences that have most affected him.

First of all, it shows vividly how much he enjoyed the chance to be with his sons and to do things with them. From his admiring words to both young men, it is clear that he thought highly of them. He taught them how to polish the car. He planned to have Biff help him chop down an overhanging branch threatening the house. He hoped to have them swing a hammock with him. He brought them a new punching bag and regaled them with his travel experiences. He was glad when they missed him when he was away and wanted their company on a summer trip along his route.

Willy is thus pictured as the devoted family man, perhaps

excessively devoted. As a traveling salesman, he was, of course, away from home a great deal. On the part of both father and sons, there is an extraordinary degree of mutual affection and concern. For strapping high school boys to claim that they missed their father every minute he was away involves either exaggeration or a somewhat unusual relationship. Willy, in turn, clearly made them his primary interest. This revelation is important because the lives of both Willy and Biff will be tragically disturbed when a break occurs between them.

Secondly, Willy is represented as a man who is capable with his hands. He gives his sons good, practical instructions about the care of the car. He suggests how they will remove the branch and how they will put up the hammock. He is also enthusiastic about this type of work and conveys pride in doing it well.

Thirdly, Willy places great stock in physical fitness. He does not bring his sons home a book or a science kit. He buys them a punching bag, excellent "for timing." He also talks of the advantages of jumping rope and is keenly interested in the coming football game.

Furthermore, Willy is convinced that popularity is a strong predictor of success. He is delighted that the girls like Biff and he is overjoyed that the coach likes Biff and that the team has chosen him captain. He suggests that the business he will someday own will be more impressive than that of their neighbor, Charley, because he, Willy, is better liked. He emphasizes this quality by telling the boys about his New England route. He has been greeted by the Mayor of Providence. He has friends in every town. Everyone likes him and will welcome his sons when he brings them along. Even the police do not ticket his car because they recognize and respect him.

Willy is bragging. He will tell Linda on another occasion that he often fears that other people are laughing at him. But even if here he is engaged in wishful thinking, it is clear that he very much wants to be highly regarded. His question as to whether or not the sons were lonesome for him indicates his desire to be well liked at home as well.

If, however, he instills in his sons the importance of personal popularity, he is not at all emphatic about the need for personal integrity. When he learns that Biff has taken the football, he tells him to return it, but he is laughing at the time and is clearly not much upset about the theft. Biff needs the ball for his practicing, and the coach will hardly disapprove. Willy feels that others might be censured, but the well-liked Biff can get away with anything. Subsequently, Biff declares he will make a special touchdown for Willy. According to Happy, Biff is not supposed to do this. He has been instructed to pass. But again Willy is delighted with the intended gesture. If Willy gives his sons values, they do not include being taught to respect the property rights or authority of others. Later we will find that Biff goes on stealing and that Happy accepts sizable bribes.

Finally, Willy once more reveals his optimistic nature. The car looks fine after the polishing, and the hammock will be hung just right. The coach will understand Biff's "borrowing" of the football and will even commend his "initiative." Someday Willy will have his own business. Meanwhile, he can take the boys on a wonderful trip. All the cities that he visits are beautiful, historic spots, with friendly, admirable people. Given even faint hopes, Willy tends to respond with enthusiasm.

BIFF

This scene emphasizes Biff's strong affection for his father, his popularity in school, and his rather questionable moral values.

Biff works hard on the car, obviously eager for Willy's praise.

He is delighted with the present of the punching bag and speaks of missing his father "every minute" while the latter was in New England. He listens appreciatively to Willy's stories and is eager to go with him on the projected summer trip. He will not be worried about the big game if his father is present. He will even go against orders to make a special touchdown just for Willy.

His popularity is suggested by the rumor Willy heard that the girls are paying to go out with him. He is also captain of the football team, and the coach, at least according to Biff, is always encouraging him. He is sure of himself and not worried at all about the stolen ball. The fact that he is so casual about admitting the theft suggests that he is not given to guilt feelings about such moral lapses. He intends to return it anyway, he says angrily, when accused. Biff's habit of taking things, shown here, will later lead him into serious trouble. He will have to leave Oliver's employ after stealing a carton of basketballs.

HAPPY

As compared with Biff, the young Happy receives little attention from Willy. Willy does tell Happy to follow Biff's lead in polishing the car, and he does throw him a word or two of praise. In general, however, Happy seems here as elsewhere to be trying to attract some attention. He lies down and pedals with his feet to show how he is losing pounds. And his "You notice, Pop?" seems to be a cry for more of Willy's regard. Willy does respond but without any continued interest. Hence, there will never be the closeness between them that develops between Willy and Biff.

CHARLEY

Willy's next-door neighbor is mentioned here as already owning his own business. Willy, however, does not seem impressed. Willy believes that Charley is not sufficiently well liked to achieve the kind of success of which Willy dreams. The contrast between the two men will be developed further in later scenes.

PLOT DEVELOPMENT

This flashback to earlier, less troubled times represents a further move toward his impending death. The painful contrast between the happy past and the troubled present will increase Willy's emotional strain. Gradually such memories will force him to live again with anguish as his relationship with Biff crumbles. The exposition shows us that Biff's later stealing becomes more comprehensible in the light of his earlier, laughingly condoned purloining of the football.

TECHNIQUE

This scene is the first of the play's now famous flashback episodes. Special lighting and a thin, transparent curtain, or scrim, are often used to distinguish these past events from those going on outside Willy's mind at the present time. There has been a lapse of some fifteen years since the car polishing and the big game actually took place. Thus all the characters in such scenes were, naturally, that much younger. Yet the same actors play the roles at both ages. The younger Linda, when she appears, will wear a ribbon in her hair. The sons, when of high-school age, will wear appropriate sweaters. Much will be suggested by the skilled use of voice and gesture. Willy, for example, hunched over with weariness when he first enters with his suitcases, will walk with a springier step and use more confident tones as the earlier, less harassed salesman.

One vital distinction must be made. To some extent the scenes from the past provide exposition—necessary information to make the present action intelligible. Yet they are part of the present action. They represent the memories that are plaguing Willy and hastening his final crack-up. Willy is collapsing mentally and emotionally, and these particular recollections, in which he loses himself completely to the horror of his family, are very real factors in his progress toward self-destruction.

How accurately do Willy's memories record what actually occurred long ago? There is evidence that Biff was once very fond of his father, that Biff was a school athlete, and that Biff did steal. Yet it is virtually impossible to determine whether or not Willy has distorted the overall picture, and if so, to what extent. All that can be stated positively is Willy's memories are valid to him. Such scenes probably reveal more about Willy's psychological processes than they do about the factual history of the Loman family.

IMPORTANT THEMES

IMPORTANCE OF BEING WELL LIKED
Willy is most enthusiastic about Biff's popularity and makes a slurring reference to Charley as not being sufficiently "well liked." Biff, being highly regarded, will get away with the football theft. Willy, being well thought of, will have a greater business success than Charley. Willy's account of his recent New England trip lays stress upon the friendly reception he is always given in the cities along his route. He intimates that popularity is the key to success.

IMPORTANCE OF PHYSICAL PROWESS
Willy buys the punching bag and tells Happy that jumping rope will help his timing. He is clearly interested in the upcoming football game. In addition, the car-polishing, branch-cutting, and hammock-slinging activities mentioned are all essentially physical.

IMPORTANCE OF FAMILY TIES
Both father and sons reveal intense affection. The boys miss Willy greatly when he is away, and are eager for his praise. He wants to take them along on his route and show them off to his New England friends. He will brag about Biff's football prowess in Boston.

QUESTIONABLE MORALITY

Willy tells Biff to return the stolen ball but tends to condone his action. For one thing, Willy feels that Biff needs the ball to practice. Secondly, the theft shows independence and daring. Finally, Biff can get away with it because the coach has a high opinion of him. In later scenes, there will be other examples in which Willy shows this same lax attitude toward obviously censurable conduct.

SYMBOLS

In various of Miller's works certain objects are used to point up significant themes.The old Chevrolet which Biff has polished is, of course, Willy's means of carrying on his job. But here it points up the close cooperation and friendly relationship between father and sons.

Together with the tree trunk that must be lopped off, the hammock first recalls the countrylike atmosphere later to disappear. The hammock is also to be one more present Willy brings home to his beloved sons. Finally, they will put it up together—hence, it is another family project.

The stolen ball, of course, ties in with Biff's preoccupation with sports. It also is used to show his dubious moral values.

ACT I, SCENE 4
SUMMARY

As Willy's memories continue, young Bernard, Charley's son, enters to warn Biff that if he does not pass mathematics he will not graduate. Willy sneers at the studious, bespectacled Bernard. Willy tells Biff to study, but is not seriously concerned. Bernard, he says, may get better marks, but Biff will be offered scholarships and succeed even as well as Willy in New England because the Lomans make a good appearance and are well liked. Happy again claims that he is losing weight by pedaling.

CHARACTER ANALYSES

WILLY

Here Willy again insists that being popular and making a good impression guarantees success. He does not tell Biff not to study. He does send him over to work with Bernard, but he is clearly convinced that the handsome, athletic Biff will get what he wants without much intellectual effort. Bernard works much more earnestly and gets much better marks. But Willy thinks that this pale, slight lad who wears glasses and is not extremely "well liked" will never have Biff's chance to forge ahead in business. As the play proceeds, it will become clear that Biff fails and Bernard succeeds. This fact will distress and bewilder Willy, but as a younger man, he is quite certain as he counsels his sons.

To make his point here Willy boasts of his own sales record in New England. Once his name is mentioned, all the buyers gladly see him. He has made great sales in Providence and Boston. Later he will admit to Linda that the trip was arduous and the returns relatively small. Why, then, does he paint here such a false picture? It is possible, of course, that in a momentary burst of enthusiasm he actually believes what he says. He is carried away with his own theory of the importance of popularity and thinks of himself as a shining example. In addition, he always seems to be courting the love and admiration of his sons, so he probably always wants to play the hero before them. With Linda, by contrast, he sometimes lowers his guard. Finally, it is at least possible that for all his bluster, Bernard's dire predictions have shaken him slightly. His scornful references to the anemic young neighbor and his glorifying of the Loman breed of muscular, personable men may be thus essentially defensive.

BIFF

Bernard says that Biff will fail mathematics and lose his chance to graduate if he does not study. Biff neither denies nor accepts this well-meant warning. Instead he seems determined to evade the issue. He shows his father how he has printed University of Virginia on one of his sneakers. He brings up the matter of Bernard's limited popularity. He also changes the subject, asking about his father's trip. He seems to have accepted Willy's values regarding the importance of being popular. He also exhibits some of Willy's dubiously grounded optimism. The name of the university is printed on his sneaker. So, of course, he is on his way. The other unpleasantness will somehow be avoided.

HAPPY

There are here two brief revealing glimpses of Happy. The first occurs when he roughly, teasingly spins the less brawny Bernard around. This is the same Happy who will later be outraged that he must take orders from weaker men whom he can outbox and outlift. Again Happy is seen pedaling and trying to get Willy to note his loss of weight. Once more Biff has been the center of attention, and Happy seems to be begging for his share.

BERNARD

In his first appearance, Bernard is a thin young man who wears glasses. He has no cause to fear about his own marks, but he is fond of Biff and worries about his friend's future.

Sneered at by Willy and taunted by Happy, he still comes to offer Biff his services as math coach. Considering the cool reception he gets, he shows remarkable patience and loyalty.

PLOT DEVELOPMENT

This memory of how he reassured Biff and spoke disdainfully of Bernard will undoubtedly help unsettle Willy still further when he later encounters Bernard as an assured, prosperous young lawyer at a time when Biff has no career at all. The matter of Biff's weakness in mathematics will also lead to the crucial subsequent Boston episode, which in turn will torment Willy and help drive him to his death.

IMPORTANT THEMES

IMPORTANCE OF BEING WELL LIKED

Biff is better looking and better liked than Bernard, says Willy. So Biff will forge far ahead of the more studious Bernard once both are out in the business world. Willy himself succeeds in New England, he claims, because people are always glad to see him. "Be liked and you will never want," he says.

IMPORTANCE OF PHYSICAL PROWESS

The scornful references to Bernard as "anemic" and to the Loman boys as "Adonises" point up Willy's concept of the advantages possessed by the man of strong physique. Happy, too, tries to claim some notice by the physical activity of pedaling and the claim of losing weight for greater fitness. Both sons, when grown, it will be remembered, make much of their muscular virility.

IMPORTANCE OF SUSTAINED EFFORT

Willy seems to have a certain contempt for Bernard's excellent marks. He dismisses him as a "pest." But the play will trace Bernard's success as contrasted with the confused floundering of all three Loman men. There is thus the implication that in the modern world, Bernard's course was the more likely to provide security, advancement, and certain other rewards.

QUESTIONABLE MORALITY
Willy seems undisturbed by the news that Biff has not been studying. The school would not dare fail anyone whose athletic achievements had led to offers of scholarships to several universities, he feels. Biff could get away with the football, so he will get away with poor grades, Willy reasons.

FAMILY SOLIDARITY
Bernard, of course, provides a contrast to Biff: notice that both men have names that start with "B." The three Lomans close ranks against him. The husky, well-liked Adonises, admiring each other, band together against the outsider.

SYMBOL: BIFF'S SNEAKERS
Biff's sports shoes, with the University of Virginia carefully printed on the sole, represent his confident dream of a bright future through athletic scholarship. When this is shattered, he will destroy the sneakers in a fit of angry bitterness.

ACT I, SCENE 5
SUMMARY

As Willy goes on remembering, he is joined by the younger Linda, carrying some wash. Willy sends the boys to hang it on the line, and Biff is helped by the school crowd whom he leads. Willy boasts to Linda of enormous sales but finally admits his commissions will not run above seventy dollars. Yet they must have over a hundred for household repairs, which leaves Willy discouraged and unsure of himself. Linda flatters him reassuringly, and he is reminded of a Boston woman with whom he had an affair. He gave her stockings and the woman promised to get him in to see the buyers.

CHARACTER ANALYSES

WILLY

Willy here is extremely proud of Biff when he hears him ordering around the other lads. He takes credit for training him to be a leader and promptly goes on to preen himself on his own extraordinary sales work. As Linda probes, however, he lowers his estimates drastically and reaches for the excuse that the stores were taking inventory. Next time, however, he will do better.

Faced with the mounting bills for the car, refrigerator, washing machine, and roof repair, Willy suddenly seems to lose all the air of bravado he puts on before the boys. He is not at all sure that everyone likes him. Some do not pay attention to him at all, and others find him ridiculous. He is afraid that he talks too much, unlike Charley for whom they do have regard. Instead of being strong and godlike, he feels pudgy and fears that he looks foolish. He must work long hours for a discouragingly small return, and he gets very lonely on the road. Recalling this loneliness, he has the guilty recollection of being unfaithful to the loyal Linda with a Boston woman.

When Willy talks like this, audiences may well wonder which

is his real personality. Is he deliberately lying to the boys? Is all the boasting a desperate attempt to mask his sense of frustration and failure? Or are these the quickly changing moods of a mercurial individual?

Certainly Willy is given to rapid shifts in judgment. In the opening scene one minute he suggests that Biff is lazy, the next that he is never lazy. In this scene he first has nothing but praise for his Chevrolet, then shortly afterwards wonders why they let such cars be assembled at all. Again within a single speech he says that he is well liked and that others do not approve of him. Since he changes opinions so quickly, it may be that his rapid transitions from hopefulness to despair are characteristic of his temperament.

As for his affair with the woman, he is not dissatisfied with Linda and does not seem proud of himself for having been unfaithful. He can usually find excuses for his actions, and here he mentally attributes his lapse to loneliness. Later he will give Biff the same reason. Yet when he is shown with the woman, he seems to be obviously enjoying himself. He relishes her flattering compliments and likes having his rather unsubtle jokes appreciated. Like Happy's conquests, the affair gives him the feeling of being a suave, irresistible man of the world. He cannot meet all the bills at home, but in Boston he can proffer a princely gift of stockings. In addition, he justifies the affair by saying that it is good business, for the woman may give him entrée to see more buyers.

LINDA

The younger, more sparkling Linda is as kind to Willy as her older self. She tells him encouragingly that his future sales will be better and makes the current ones sound as good as possible. She assures him that he is good-looking and commends his lively talk. Yet, however soothing her words, she is never unaware of the harsh economic facts. She knows exactly, dollar for dollar, what things cost and what Willy brings in. When Willy talks grandly of selling thousands, her quick, instinctive query is, "Did you sell anything?" Intent upon figuring the commission so that she can pay off bills, she forces him to admit failure. But she recovers quickly and works to restore his confidence. Some critics have suggested that had the faithful Linda been more direct and less soothing, she might have helped Willy act more maturely.

BIFF

Right before the big game, Biff is portrayed as the idol of the neighborhood boys. They wait around in the Loman cellar and gladly execute his orders to sweep the furnace room or hang up the wash. Both Biff and his brother are good-natured about helping out at home. They gaily agree to take over the chores from Linda.

PLOT DEVELOPMENT

This is one more pleasant memory of family happiness and cooperation, which makes the current tensions with Biff more disturbing. In addition, this memory recalls Biff's moment of glory as the leader among the boys, as contrasted to Biff's present status as an insignificant drifter. At the same time, the scene has its darker side. Willy is remembering that even in his prime, he was never much of a success. He is haunted by the Boston affair that made him feel guilty about his disloyalty to Linda and that led to his troubles with Biff. This scene thus contains various elements that help to increase Willy's current anxieties.

TECHNIQUE

The episode is a flashback. Within this memory, however, there is an additional one. Willy at present recalls his past conversation with Linda. At the time he had that talk, he was reminded of a previous encounter with the woman in Boston. Special musical effects, lighting, and scrim make the necessary distinctions onstage.

IMPORTANT THEMES

IMPORTANCE OF BEING WELL LIKED

Willy is delighted here because Biff clearly is popular with the boys, who regard him as their leader. Willy sees here the proof of his theory of success. As for himself, when he is worried about his own lack of progress, he is afraid that he is not well enough liked.

FAMILY SOLIDARITY

The boys gladly help out with the wash or get the furnace room swept. Linda and Willy talk of paying off household bills. Willy, seeing Linda and appreciating her love, is distressed to remember his disloyalty.

THE HARD STRUGGLE OF THE AVERAGE FAMILY

There is much detailed reference here to nagging bills for car, roof, and household appliances. Willy talks of the long hours of work necessary to make even fair commissions. *Death of a Salesman* is sometimes described as a tragedy of the "little man" or the "common man." Here the modest sums needed, that are so difficult for this family to raise, point up the low-income status of this man with grand visions.

QUESTIONABLE MORALITY

Both Happy and Biff have been seen earlier as unmarried men who have had affairs with women. Their ideal, however, has been a stable marriage with a good, steady girl like Linda. Willy hitherto has been his sons' hero as good husband and good father. Here, however, he is shown to be guilty of marital infidelity. His excuse is loneliness. As before, the audience is made aware that Willy's moral standards can be curiously flexible.

SYMBOLS

The apron, hair ribbon, and basket of wash symbolize the housewife. Linda here is contrasted with the "other woman" in the hotel room. The stockings stand for infidelity. They represent Willy's attempt to look impressive outside the home. Linda darns her own stockings. Given the economic straits of the Loman home, new stockings are a luxury.

ACT I, SCENE 6
SUMMARY

In the continued memory episode, Willy is watching Linda darn her stockings. Willy angrily tells her to throw them out. Bernard comes in with a new warning about Biff's failing. Willy also hears that Biff is being too forward with girls and is driving without a license. Willy does not want a spineless nonentity like Bernard, who will not cheat for Biff on final exams, but neither can he understand where Biff has gotten some of his dubious values.

CHARACTER ANALYSES

WILLY

Willy is greatly disturbed by references to Biff's youthful wildness. Willy does not want Biff to steal or cheat or act in an ungentlemanly manner. He even threatens to beat him to make him stop. Yet Willy, Biff's idol, did describe his taking of the football as "initiative." Even now Willy is pleading with Bernard to give Biff answers on the final statewide Regents examinations, so there is irony in Willy's wondering where Biff could have learned such wrong ideas. His father always gave him "decent" standards.

BIFF

Despite Bernard's warnings, Biff has not been studying. Instead he is driving without a license and being rough with the girls. Also he has not returned the football. The only explanation offered for such behavior is Bernard's report that a teacher considers Biff "stuck up." Willy has long been praising Biff and encouraging him to think well of himself. Biff has apparently become a very confident youth, certain that he can breeze through life doing what he pleases.

BERNARD

Bernard is anxious about Biff and willing to help him before the test. He refuses, however, to run the risk of being caught on an important final examination. Bernard, apparently, is not altogether above some dishonesty on behalf of a friend. He has, in the past, given Biff some answers. But Bernard is not one to jeopardize his future, either, so he refuses Willy's plea and is angrily silenced by the irate salesman.

PLOT DEVELOPMENT

Here Willy's shining confidence in Biff is put to the test, and Willy characteristically tries to make excuses and even deny the truth. These memories, however, are distressing ones. Biff is riding for a fall, and his school difficulties will eventually lead to the break between him and Willy. The memory of this break and the events leading up to it weigh heavily upon the older Willy's confused mind.

TECHNIQUE

This scene is a flashback, without the overlapping effect of the previous scene. The only variation occurs when the Boston woman's laugh is heard half-mockingly amidst Willy's angry attempts to silence Biff's accusers. Willy seems particularly upset about Biff's rough behavior toward girls. The woman's laugh constitutes a reminder of his own unauthorized romance. It also looks ahead to the crucial break with Biff that will occur when Willy is discovered with her in compromising circumstances.

IMPORTANT THEMES

IMPORTANCE OF BEING WELL LIKED

Even when Willy is alarmed about Biff's behavior, he still retorts that Biff has "spirit" and personality, in contrast to insignificant types like Bernard.

QUESTIONABLE MORALITY

Willy threatens to punish Biff for stealing and misbehaving with the girls. But Willy also urges Bernard to give Biff answers dishonestly on the final examination.

FATHER-SON SOLIDARITY

Even though he does not appear to be at all certain that Biff has acted admirably, Willy rudely silences Linda and angrily sends Bernard home.

SYMBOLS

The football is mentioned again, pointing up Biff's tendency to steal. Linda says that it should be returned. Willy furiously denies that this was stealing at all. After all, Biff is bringing it back. The stockings represent Willy's infidelity. Willy irately demands that Linda throw away the stockings she is darning. Seeing her mending them makes him feel like a poor provider. He also has a sense of guilt, since he gave a box of stockings to the Boston woman. Characteristically, Willy mainly does not want to see Linda darning. Both he and Biff prefer to evade unpleasant reminders. Yet the memory scenes indicate that even when he can have disturbing matters removed from view, Willy can not get them out of his mind.

ACT I, SCENE 7
SUMMARY

Back in the present, Happy comes down to coax Willy to bed. Willy laments that he never went to Alaska with his successful brother Ben and sneers at Happy's offer to finance his retirement. Charley comes over. They play cards, and Willy scorns his friend as ignorant about vitamins and carpentry. He also proudly turns down his offer of a job. Willy then seems to see the long-dead adventurous Ben. He talks confusedly with both his vision and the bewildered Charley. Soon he insults Charley once more, and Charley resignedly goes home.

CHARACTER ANALYSES

WILLY

Apparently much disturbed by the previous recollections, Willy acts irritably toward both Happy and Charley. He ridicules Happy's fine-sounding offer to "retire him for life." He knows how much his son makes and how much he spends on car, apartment, and women. Willy is not usually one to face facts squarely, but he recognizes here that his "woods are burning"—his situation is desperate. He finds no comfort in Happy's soothing assurances.

As for the affronts to Charley, there are three possible explanations. First of all, Willy is edgy with everybody. In the first scene he was irked because Linda bought a new type of cheese. Secondly, despite his kindliness, Charley always increases Willy's sense of failure. Charley has a flourishing business and a successful son. Finally, Willy keeps trying to see himself and his sons as superior beings. Charley could never put up a ceiling, but Willy is good with his hands. He finally angers even the unexcitable Charley by his rash statement that since Charley is unable to handle tools, Charley is not much of a man. But this hostile remark is in line with Willy's overall stress upon those skills that he and his sons can claim to possess.

This scene also brings out Willy's admiration for his older brother Ben, who made a fortune in the jungle when he was young. To Willy, Ben stands for success through vision and determination. Ben knew what he wanted, went after it, and got it. He knew how to take advantage of opportunities in Alaska and Africa. Willy now feels that he should have gone with him, for then he would be rich. Ben represents the American dream of rising by one's own efforts from poverty and obscurity to great wealth. Ben makes the daring move and realizes the ambition. Willy stays with the same small job, bragging about the past and making great predictions about the future. Ben is dream plus action; Willy is merely dream.

CHARLEY

Charley is the amiable, understanding neighbor who sees that Willy is distraught and wants to calm him down. He comes to play cards with him in the middle of the night in the hope of making him tired enough to sleep. He offers him a job even though he takes considerable abuse from the short-tempered, uneasy Willy. Yet Charley does not lack spirit. He answers Willy quite sharply when the latter suggests that his inability to handle tools makes him less of a man. Indeed, Charley's suddenly authoritative tone reminds Willy of the brisk, assertive manner of his determined brother, Ben.

Just as Charley's son, Bernard, contrasts with Biff, so Charley contrasts to Willy. Charley is unassuming and unpretentious, but generally well adjusted and relatively successful. Over the years Charley's family has lived next door. The two homes, and hence the general economic background, are presumably similar. Charley, however, has not demanded as much from life as Willy, and, paradoxically, has apparently received more.

Charley and Willy are also contrasted as fathers. Here Willy confides in his friend that he is distressed about Biff's plan to return West. Willy is particularly saddened to think that since he is short of money, he cannot give Biff anything. Charley feels that a thirty-four-year old son should be left to shift for himself. He urges Willy to let Biff go and "forget him." But Willy cannot do this, for his whole life is centered in his son. Later Charley and Bernard will visit on easy, friendly terms, man to man. By letting his son go, Charley keeps his pleasant relationship. Willy holds on, at least in his mind, and makes Biff and himself miserable.

HAPPY

Happy also tries to calm Willy. Always one to gloss over unpleasantness, he attempts to halt Willy's regrets about the past and to assure Charley that nothing is wrong. He is interested, however, in the legend of get-rich-quick Uncle Ben. Like his father, Happy dreams of making an impressive coup. But when he assures Willy that he will finance his retirement, Willy snorts. He may not be able to recognize his own meaningless boasts, but he can puncture Happy's. So again Happy is shown to be the less favored son.

BEN

Since Ben is seen only as one of Willy's disturbing memories, it is hard to know how far the vision represents a real person. Willy does tell Charley that his brother died recently in Africa and left seven sons. But Ben, as he appears from Willy's recollections, is a curious figure. He stands for two concepts. First of all, he is rejected opportunity. Had Willy gone with him to Alaska, Willy might have had a great fortune. Second, he is the cold, ruthless, triumphant victor over life's jungle. Ben knows what he wants and lets nothing interfere. He is daring and unscrupulous in a way Willy could never be. There may well have been such a person. But some critics at least have wondered whether or not "Ben" was essentially a personification summing up certain of Willy's aspirations. He may well be the wild, adventurous pioneer that the more domesticated salesman at times wishes he could have been.

PLOT DEVELOPMENT

Here it becomes evident that Willy's crack-up cannot be kept within the family. Charley can hear his noisy, rambling talk from next door. Charley also hears him talk confusedly to an unseen Ben. Another interesting development is Charley's offer of a job. Whatever is disturbing Willy, the solution cannot be found in mere economic security. Pride, of course, enters into his angry rejection of Charley's offer, but this only further indicates that Willy's sad decline is essentially a matter of inner tensions and anxieties.

TECHNIQUE

In this scene there is an even more startling use of combined objective events and Willy's mental figments. At one point, Willy is conversing both with the actually present Charley and his vision of the now dead Ben. As a stage effect this is striking. There is some humor here as Charley tries to make sense out of this strange triangular parley. But it also serves to point up Willy's deteriorating condition.

IMPORTANT THEMES

SUCCESS THROUGH DARING VENTURES

Ben went into the jungle as a young man and came out with a fortune in diamonds. He never had to "grub for money." Willy regrets he never went off with Ben to Alaska for a similar rapidly acquired windfall.

FATHER-SON SOLIDARITY

Charley urges Willy to let Biff go and not worry about him further. Willy cannot do this. He wishes only that he had more to give Biff.

IMPORTANCE OF PHYSICAL PROWESS

Willy sneers bitterly at Charley for his inability to handle tools. Their manual skills always make the Loman men feel superior.

SYMBOLS

Ben's African cache of diamonds always represents to Willy the wealth to be obtained by vision and determination.

Like the hammock, the overhanging bough, and the roof, the newly installed ceiling is used to symbolize Willy's skill with his hands, a type of work of which the more financially successful Charley is totally incapable. Throughout there is the suggestion that the Lomans have certain aptitudes that cannot be used remuneratively in the urban job area where they seek success.

ACT I, SCENE 8
SUMMARY

Alone again, Willy relives Ben's one visit to Brooklyn. Ben and their father had gone off separately when Willy was a baby in South Dakota. Their father, says Ben, was a bold, adventurous man, who toured the land selling handmade flutes. Ben alarms Linda by urging Biff never to fight fairly with strangers, but Willy calls him a great man. To fix the stoop, Willy sends Biff to steal sand from the apartment builders. They have already taken lumber. Charley and Bernard enter and decry this thievery but they are ridiculed. As Ben leaves, he again tells Willy's sons how he made a fast fortune. He also reassures Willy that he is bringing his boys up well.

CHARACTER ANALYSES

WILLY

This scene again emphasizes Willy's strong family feelings. He welcomes Ben and wants to hear more of their father. He is also eager to show how well he works with his boys by repairing the stoop while Ben waits. Again Willy shows his contempt for Charley and Bernard because they cannot work so well with their hands. Again he reveals dubious moral values by encouraging Biff's stealing. At the same time, his anxious questions to Ben about his sons show the uncertainty that plagued even the younger, more assured Willy.

BEN

Ben has a courtly graciousness as he greets Linda, but he can also be frightening. As he shows Biff how to fight, he trips him and poises his umbrella point over the boy's eye. Also, he is not disturbed about the stolen lumber. His sense of family responsibility also seems never to have been very strong. It appears that when he left the wagon in South Dakota as a lad of seventeen, he walked off from his mother and the very young Willy, the father having already deserted them to head for Alaska. This is his one visit to Willy, and he has to ask if their mother is still alive. Ben, however, is completely sure of himself and proud of his quickly acquired fortune in diamonds. He has never kept books, and some of his enterprises may have been questionable. But to the uncertain, struggling Willy he exudes success, and is therefore a "great man."

LINDA

Linda is not favorably impressed by Ben. She does not like Ben's insisting that Biff fight and she is horrified when he trips the boy, menaces him with the tip of his umbrella, and warns him against fighting too fairly with strangers. Linda is also worried when Biff is chased by the watchman after stealing some sand. In general, Linda's standards seem somewhat higher than Willy's. But her protests tend to be mild. Her "Biff, dear!" as she runs off, alarmed, does not sound as if she were about to be sternly unforgiving.

CHARLEY

Looking somewhat absurd in knickers, Charley comes over to warn Willy about Biff's risk of being arrested. Charley is always the good neighbor, as is his son who comes to announce that Biff is being chased by the watchman. As usual, however, the well-meant efforts of both are scornfully repulsed. Again, too, the point is made that neither can hammer nails.

BIFF

Again the young Biff is shown eager to obey his father and to work with him on the stoop. He also is not at all annoyed that Willy should ask him to steal. Willy says that he and Happy are "fearless characters," with Biff possessing "nerves of iron." Such praise seems to be encouraging them to have little respect for the property rights of others.

PLOT DEVELOPMENT

Willy's memories of Ben's impressively rapid acquisition of enormous wealth will later be influential in Willy's debate with himself about committing suicide for the insurance money.

Also Biff's stealing, with parental encouragement, will help to make the later Oliver episode more catastrophic.

TECHNIQUE
This is a straight flashback scene with no interweaving of action in the present.

IMPORTANT THEMES

FAMILY SOLIDARITY
Willy admires his brother and wants to hear more of their father, whom Ben describes with enthusiasm. Willy is proud that his sons are "rugged, well liked, and fearless." Ben praises Willy as a good father to his "manly" sons.

QUESTIONABLE MORALITY
Willy encourages the boys to steal sand and lumber from the construction company. He does not protest when Ben encourages Biff to fight unfairly.

IMPORTANCE OF PHYSICAL PROWESS
Willy is eager to show how he and the boys can fix the stoop. He also claims that Biff can cut down a tree. He sneers at the neighbors who cannot hammer nails.

IMPORTANCE OF BEING WELL LIKED
Willy tells Ben that he is bringing his boys up to be popular. Ben approves of his training.

SUCCESS THROUGH DARING VENTURES
Willy holds Ben up to the boys as a great man because he made a large and seemingly easy fortune in the jungle. Ben praises his father because through gadgets he made more money in one week than Willy could in all his life. This is undoubtedly nonsense, but Biff has said that he was never brought up to "grub for money." Ben seems again to be stressing the quick return.

SYMBOLS

The younger Linda, entering with the wash, seems to personify the settled domestic life as against Ben's invitation to adventurous doings in far-off lands. Linda is hostile to Ben.

Biff fondly recalls Willy repairing the stoop. It represents Willy's expert manual skills and his interest in the home. It is also Willy's limited answer to Ben. If he has not found a fortune in diamonds, he can at least fix a stoop. Yet even this irreproachable activity is tied in with Biff's stealing and with mean sneers at the less handy neighbors.

Charley wears knickers that his wife picked out for him. Here the outfit contrasts Charley as a hen-pecked man who cannot work with his hands with the more assertive Loman men who have such skills. Charley and Bernard are worried about the thefts and are clearly not "fearless characters." The contrast between the families is always somewhat ironic, but here the knickers give Willy one more chance to voice ridicule and contempt.

In Willy's visions, Ben is always looking at his watch and hurrying off. Never having seen much of father or brother, Willy is always pleading for more help and never getting more than a few terse statements. Ben is an elusive memory. In a sense, too, his watch seems to point up the need for quick decisions when an opportunity presents itself. Willy thinks of himself as having had only one brief chance to reach for untold wealth. He missed it. He will later see a second such chance in the suicide plan.

ACT I, SCENE 9
SUMMARY

The vision of Ben fades, and Willy is rejoined by Linda, who reminds him that they long ago pawned Ben's diamond watch-fob gift to pay for Biff's correspondence course. In his slippers, Willy goes out for a walk. The boys come down, and Linda says that Willy is worse whenever Biff returns. Biff promises to reform. Linda speaks lovingly of Willy, saying that he is old and worn but deserves respect. Despite his long service, the company has put him back on straight commission, and so he secretly borrows money from Charley to meet his bills. She accuses her sons of neglect. She adds that Willy plans suicide. Once he smashed the car, and he still hides a rubber tube for inhaling gas in the cellar. The boys are horrified. Biff promises to once again tackle the business world, but thinks all three would be better off as carpenters working in the open air.

CHARACTER ANALYSES

WILLY

This scene emphasizes Willy's disturbed state. He insists upon going out late at night in his slippers. More alarmingly, he has actually tried suicide. Linda also points out that he has been a good, hard-working man deserving of some consideration. She also stresses his continued concern for his undeserving sons.

LINDA

Linda speaks affectionately and admiringly of Willy but she is not completely blind to his limitations. She has to admit that he is not easy to live with. She knows that he deceives her about the gas device. She admits that he is not a "great man" or even the "finest character." If she is to this extent clear-sighted about Willy, she is even more harsh in judging the boys. She chides them for their neglect, tells Biff to treat his father more respectfully, and speaks scornfully of Happy as a

"philandering bum." She condemns both her sons as ungrateful and will not permit them to sympathize with her if it means
attacking Willy. She may patiently soothe and encourage Willy,
but to the boys she can be spirited, sharp, and uncompromising. Either Biff behaves himself or he leaves the house, she
says.

BIFF

Biff is confused and upset in this scene. He is fond of his
mother and eager to please her. At the same time he obviously has some grudge against Willy, whom she so staunchly
defends. He feels guilty when Linda tells him that his coming
home causes Willy to become more agitated. Yet if Willy needs
help, Biff must stay around and get a job. He obviously hates
the business world and feels ill at ease about trying to reenter
it. Yet as Linda talks of Willy's misfortunes and his need for
help, Biff feels miserable and promises to help. Throughout
he appears to be goodhearted but very uncertain as to his
course.

HAPPY

As usual, Happy tries ineffectually to make everything seem
all right. He tries to reassure Linda that Biff really is devoted
to Willy. He also claims, in opposition to Biff, that Willy has
treated Linda with consideration. He is sure that the insurance
company was wrong in suggesting that Willy's car crashes
were intentional. When, however, Biff turns on him, he
answers angrily, defending Willy against his brother. Yet even
he is disgusted when he learns that Willy is concealing the
gas-inhaling tube.

PLOT DEVELOPMENT

The story Linda tells of Willy's desperate plight motivates Biff
more strongly to try to get a loan from Oliver. The references
to the suicide attempts help to prepare for Willy's final self-
destructive course.

TECHNIQUE

Except for the scene in the boys' bedroom, this is the first scene in which Willy is not present. The central role is a demanding one, for Willy is on the stage most of the time. Many of the scenes in which he figures involve memories that may or may not be distorted. This scene takes place in the present without flashbacks.

IMPORTANT THEMES

CORRUPTION IN MODERN BUSINESS

Willy has worked for almost thirty-six years for the company. During that time he has opened up new markets and served them faithfully. The company, however, shows no gratitude. As his production slows up with increasing age, he is deprived of a steady salary and put back on straight commission like a beginner. The treatment, as Linda sees it, is inhuman and plays havoc with a man's self-respect. Linda also notes the lack of a personal element in business now. In the past old friends used to help Willy with an occasional extra order. Now he is neither known nor welcomed.

Finally, Biff admits that he has never liked the business world. Happy says that is because he never tried to please people and because he has acted irresponsibly. Biff, it seems, used to whistle in elevators. He also took days off to go swimming, but without playing Happy's game of having others lie for him. These comments can be seen as objections to the regimentation and routine of the business world, although it must be conceded that Biff and Happy are not altogether reliable critics.

FAMILY SOLIDARITY

Linda strongly affirms her love for Willy and demands that the two sons help him or be considered as ungrateful as the company. Happy's fifty-dollar Christmas gift is scornfully judged to be insufficient. The boys accept Linda's view, and Biff promises to get a job and give his father half his paycheck.

QUESTIONABLE MORALITY
Happy claims that Biff used to take time off for swimming and thus failed to make a good impression on employers. Happy's system is to go off when he pleases but to have others lie about his whereabouts. Clearly, both boys have questionable values.

COUNTRY VERSUS CITY
When working in the city, Biff could not whistle in an elevator without being thought mad. Biff wishes that he, his father, and his brother could work as carpenters out on the open prairie. Then they would be free from the "nuthouse" city and free to whistle. As devotees of the outdoor life, both brothers, apparently, have skipped work on summer days to go swimming.

FATHER-SON CONFLICT
Biff is saddened to learn of Willy's plight but still harbors some deep personal resentment. His pledge to help Willy comes half from a sense of duty and half from a desire to please the adamant Linda.

SYMBOLS
Ben's prized gift of a diamond watch fob went to pay for Biff's course. Willy will later think a great deal of Ben and diamonds when he plans another grand gesture to save Biff.

Willy's car, hitherto a means of earning his livelihood, is now seen as a possible suicide device, and it will later be used as such.

The rubber tube also signifies Willy's urge toward self-destruction, but Linda's respect for Willy will not let her destroy it.

ACT I, SCENE 10
SUMMARY

Willy returns, angered to hear Biff reduce them to carpenters. He sneers at Biff until he hears of the scheme to borrow money from Oliver. Then with enthusiasm he gives much contradictory advice. Happy says that the Loman Brothers, as a team, could sell sporting goods. Excited over the idea, Willy is rude to Linda, thus infuriating Biff. Yet Biff agrees to soothe Willy before going up to bed. Biff is suddenly confident about the future.

CHARACTER ANALYSES

WILLY

In this scene, Willy is rude and unreasonable. He is angry and possibly frightened because Biff has said that people laugh at Willy. So he must reassert himself as the "big shot" and set Biff down. Also, he is either muddled in his thinking or, as before, very changeable. He tells Biff one moment to act dignified and reserved with Oliver, the next to start the interview with some lively stories.

When he hears about the Oliver plan and also Happy's idea of the Loman Brothers business, he is immediately hopeful and enthusiastic. Yet his very optimism and feverish excitement make him even more rude and arrogant, and so the battle flares up anew.

BIFF

Although driven to defend himself, Biff tries to be patient, probably out of respect for his mother. Only when Willy harshly silences his wife does Biff completely lose his temper. In this scene, however, there is also the old assured Biff. However slim are his actual chances with Oliver, Biff, like his father and brother, has high hopes.

LINDA

At this point Linda is essentially a buffer, or peacemaker between father and son.

HAPPY

The younger son, too, tries to quell the hot tempers of Willy and Biff. He also here reveals a creative idea of his own. The brothers will team up to demonstrate and sell sports equipment. Like other Loman schemes, this is wildly impractical in view of their lack of athletic fame and money. As eager as the other two, Happy says that such a partnership would permit a friendly arrangement based upon mutual trust, not cutthroat competition. And they could also take time off to go swimming. Happy's vision is brash and boyish, but then all the Loman men are to some extent immature.

PLOT DEVELOPMENT

This scene raises the hopes of all, despite personal clashes, and sends Biff off with assurance to call on Oliver. The failure of the project will plunge Willy more deeply into despair.

IMPORTANT THEMES

FAMILY SOLIDARITY

Happy wants to work with Biff and will help him prepare for the interview. Happy and Linda try to keep peace in the family. Willy, in more tractable moments, tries to give Biff helpful advice and encouragement.

FATHER-SON CONFLICT

Willy resents what he considers Biff's contempt for him as being laughable. Willy also objects to Biff's rough talk, and Biff in turn all but accuses his father of hypocrisy. Biff also takes Linda's part when Willy shouts at her.

CORRUPTION OF MODERN BUSINESS

Happy would like to have Biff as his business partner, for then there would be "honor" and those friendly ties missing in the business world as Happy knows it. They would also have more personal freedom, for example, to go swimming without always being afraid that someone else would take advantage of them.

ACT I, SCENE 11
SUMMARY

Preparing for bed, Willy complains about the defective shower, but his hopes for Biff are now high. Both sons come to bid him good night, and he again loads Biff with dubious advice. He thinks of Biff at his moment of greatness when the fans cheered at Ebbets field. Linda soothes him with a lullaby, and he agrees to see Howard in the morning and ask for a New York assignment. Meanwhile, Biff, smoking downstairs, finds and removes the rubber tubing Willy had hidden away as a suicide device.

CHARACTER ANALYSES

WILLY

Willy continues in a highly excitable condition. He also has the optimistic notion that Biff's football success will be matched when he sees Oliver. After all, Biff has a greatness about him. Ironically, he warns Biff not to act subservient, but that is just how he himself will act with Howard, his boss.

BIFF

Troubled about Willy and yet desirous of pleasing Linda, Biff comes to say good night. Again Willy irritates him, but he controls his anger. Later he is appalled to find the rubber tubing.

LINDA

Again Linda acts with almost maternal solicitude for Willy, even singing him a lullaby. However, she also takes advantage of his hopefulness about Biff to urge him to go to see Howard. All through this and the last scene, she patiently accepts Willy's rudeness with remarkably good grace.

HAPPY

Happy tries to make noise enough to prevent another outbreak. He also assures Linda that he is getting married.

This seems a bid for attention, much like his earlier claims to Willy that he was losing weight. And it elicits the same very limited notice.

PLOT DEVELOPMENT
Linda seizes the moment of Willy's optimism regarding Biff to press him to approach Howard for an easier job. Willy listens to her and agrees to go the following morning. This crucial interview on the same day as Biff's attempt to see Oliver will accelerate Willy's downfall. In addition, Biff finding the tubing will intensify the young man's anxiety and strain, thus making his failure to convince Oliver seem the more devastating to him.

TECHNIQUE
Although there is no flashback here in the usual sense, an interesting effect is secured with lights. As Willy recalls Biff's day of triumph on the football field, he compares him to the Greek god Hercules, known for his strength. Linda, in turn, remembers his gold uniform. Meanwhile Biff stands on the lower stage level, outside the house, smoking. A gold light is then played upon him, and the audience sees him looking very much like Willy's bright image of his son at an earlier age. Lighting is also used to call attention to the gas heater, behind which Biff finds the length of tubing.

IMPORTANT THEMES

IMPORTANCE OF PHYSICAL PROWESS
To Willy, Biff must have greatness in him because he was an outstanding football player.

FAMILY SOLIDARITY
The boys come in to bid Willy good night in hopes of soothing him and reestablishing general harmony.

FATHER-SON CONFLICT
Biff remains quiet, but he is obviously irked by his father's excited counsel.

QUESTIONABLE MORALITY
Willy urges Biff to lie to Oliver about his experience out West.

SYMBOLS
Linda knows about the tubing, but will not remove it lest she hurt Willy's pride. Biff, however, is not so sensitive on this score. In hopes of staving off such a disaster, he takes the tubing away. Later, however, in the midst of a furious battle with his father, he will refer to it as a symbol of his father's weakness.

ACT II

ACT II, SCENE 1
SUMMARY

The next morning Willy, rested and hopeful, breakfasts with Linda. He talks of buying a house in the country and building guest houses. Linda asks him to get a two-hundred-dollar advance from Howard. This will pay off the mortgage after twenty-five years. She then tells him Biff and Happy have invited him to dinner that night. He leaves in high spirits. Biff calls, and Linda encourages him and tells him to be kind to Willy.

CHARACTER ANALYSES

WILLY

Here, Willy hits his final peak of confidence. Buoyed up by the boys' hopes, as well as his own, he is sure that he can persuade Howard to give him a better position in the company. He is somewhat discouraged to hear how much they owe. By the time they pay off refrigerator and car, both are worn out. But he shares Linda's satisfaction in making a final payment on the house after a quarter of a century. This scene also shows the Willy who enjoys working with his hands. He talks with pride of the repairs he has made in the house, and he looks forward to building guest houses for his sons when they move to a home in the country. Finally, his deep affection for the boys is evident. He is overjoyed that they have invited him to dinner.

LINDA

In this scene Linda is her usual encouraging self, but even she seems more than usually optimistic, caught up apparently in her husband and sons' happy mood. As before, she has no illusions about their needs. In nudging Willy again to see Howard, she reels off the exact amounts that they require for insurance, car repair, refrigerator, and mortgage payments.

Yet in view of what she knows about the company that put the aging Willy back on straight commission, she seems remarkably naive in urging him to ask for a two-hundred-dollar advance. At this point she sounds like Biff setting out to ask for ten to fifteen thousand dollars from a man he once robbed. Her deep love for Willy, however, is also evident throughout and especially during the telephone conversation with Biff. She tells him to greet his father affectionately, for Willy is "only a little boat looking for a harbor."

PLOT DEVELOPMENT
The optimistic mood here sends the hitherto beaten and despairing Willy off to make demands upon Howard. At the same time, in view of Linda's description of the family's heavy debts, it is clear that this is a last desperate chance for Willy, as is the Oliver scheme for Biff. Hence if the plea is refused, as it well may be, the consequences are likely to be grave.

TECHNIQUE
This is straight present-day conversation between Willy and Linda, but sprightly, hopeful background music is used to emphasize the mood of early-morning optimism.

IMPORTANT THEMES

COUNTRY VERSUS CITY
Willy looks forward to a house in the country where he can grow things again. He also wants to build a guest house or two there. They can raise chickens and have a vegetable garden. This would be the good life.

THE HARD STRUGGLE OF THE AVERAGE FAMILY
Much is made here of the painfully slow business of paying on the installment plan for household appliances and the car and keeping everything in repair. Insurance premiums must be met before the grace period expires, and mortgage payments must be met over a quarter of a century. Willy has

never been the illustrious figure he sometimes tries to picture himself as, but he has until recently met his obligations.

FAMILY SOLIDARITY

Linda encourages both Willy and Biff. Willy expresses high hopes for Biff. The boys want to entertain their father at dinner.

SYMBOLS

Willy sees Linda about to darn stockings and asks her not to do so while he is around. The fact that he gave stockings to the Boston woman will be brought up again significantly in a future scene.

Discovering the rubber tubing is missing from its usual place, Linda has hopefully concluded that Willy has given up the idea of suicide. She is, therefore, somewhat deflated to hear that Biff has taken it.

Willy talks often of happier days when there was more light and air and they could grow flowers and vegetables. Now, feeling hopeful, he plans to buy seeds to try again. Whether it be through plants or sons, Willy wants a sense of starting something that will develop fully in the future. His one regret about the house, now practically paid for, is that strangers will take it over after he and Linda can no longer occupy it.

ACT II, SCENE 2
SUMMARY

At the office, Howard ignores Willy. Howard is busy playing with his tape recorder. Reminding Howard of a Christmas party pledge of an office job, he vainly requests sixty-five or even fifty dollars a week. Coldly refused, he talks glowingly of the good old days, when Dave Singleman, aged eighty-four, could still take orders by phone since business was then on a friendly, man-to-man basis. Willy adds that Howard's father promised him advancement and decries Howard's failure to honor commitments. Impatiently, Howard leaves, and Willy panics when he accidentally turns on the recorder. Howard returns, and despite Willy's pleas to be allowed to go back to Boston, discharges him altogether.

CHARACTER ANALYSES

WILLY

Begging for smaller and smaller sums just to keep going, he seems a pitiable, broken old man. Gradually, however, his anger restores his dignity. Outraged by Howard's cold indifference, he cries, "You can't eat the orange and throw the peel away." His demand to be treated as a human being is a moving one. His subsequent shouting recalls the disturbed Willy of earlier scenes, but his nostalgic references to his family and to old Dave Singleman give him a strong human appeal in opposition to Howard's impersonal efficiency.

HOWARD

The impatient young executive is no conventional villain. As compared with the sensual Happy, he is the solid, respectable husband and father. He enjoys listening to his small son's voice on the new tape recorder, and he thinks of using the gadget to make sure that he does not miss the Jack Benny program, a comedy show. Yet to Howard, "business is business." He will talk pleasantly enough to employees, but if they do not bring in profits, they are expendable. He has no interest whatsoever in Willy's past record, his association with his father, or with pledges made years ago. Nor does he care how much Willy needs to feed his family. Willy's problems are his own affair. Howard's only concern is with the efficient operation of his firm. He represents the cold, practical impersonality of modern business.

PLOT DEVELOPMENT

Although Willy's confidence was high when he left Linda, he loses assurance rapidly, and even though his plea has a certain simple eloquence, he is clearly not going to be able to talk to Howard. This scene, therefore, leaves little doubt that Willy has lost his one chance. From now on, unless, of course, Biff accomplishes his improbable mission, Willy's progress will be unmistakably downhill.

IMPORTANT THEMES

CORRUPTION OF MODERN BUSINESS

Willy has worked for over thirty years for the Wagner Company. Even though "business is business," his plea of slightly more consideration as a human being is wrenching and serves to underscore the corruption of modern business.

LAMENT FOR THE PAST

Willy remembers with pride his father's and his brother's self-reliance and adventurous streaks. He also recalls the respect and friendship with which old Dave Singleman was treated as an aging salesman, and the warm association between himself and Howard's father.

SYMBOLS

The tape recorder associates Howard with a small-minded, gadget-ridden race of second-generation businessmen. He obviously lacks his father's vision and basic generosity. His pleasure is in the mechanical, and he has about him little of the humane.

DAVE SINGLEMAN

Eighty-four-year-old Dave Singleman, taking orders by telephone from his hotel room while relaxing in his green velvet slippers, represents what Willy thought and hoped would be his reward for years of hard work selling. Dave is the "single man," the individual, as contrasted to Willy's "low-man," or commonplace person.

ACT II, SCENE 3
SUMMARY

Seeing Ben again in his mind, Willy asks how he succeeded. He then recalls a past visit, in which Ben proposed that he go to Alaska. Linda, young again, carrying the wash, counters that Willy makes enough selling to be happy without leaving. She talks of Wagner's promises and of old Dave. Ben is skeptical, but Willy points to young Biff, the football hero, with scholarship offers. Willy and Biff will get their "diamonds" through being well liked by business contracts. Ben leaves.

CHARACTER ANALYSES

WILLY

Willy is indecisive. He wants to take Ben's offer of work supervising Alaskan timberland, but he listens when Linda talks of his great future in selling. He is convinced that selling is his best choice because he sees Biff already on the road to success, entirely on the basis of being well liked. Of course, Willy here is unduly optimistic even about Biff, since the scholarship offers from the three universities are contingent upon Biff's passing all his subjects.

BEN

Always in a hurry, Ben talks of fighting for a fortune on the Alaskan frontier as opposed to the slow, discouraging progress made in cities. Cities have law courts, and Ben is not one to put up with hampering restrictions. He also likes the material satisfaction of owning property. He has no use for Willy's idea that building contacts will mean future security. Ben has vision, but he is also hard, practical, and ruthless.

LINDA

Seen again with the wash, Linda defends her settled domestic domain against Ben's disturbing challenge to Willy. Linda dislikes Ben and all that he represents. She talks of Willy's popularity and of his future with the firm. She recalls old Dave Singleman, always one of Willy's ideals, and she denies that one must conquer the world in order to attain true happiness. She fights for her home and she wins.

PLOT DEVELOPMENT

Discharged by Howard, Willy is bitter and bewildered. Remembering the past when he turned down Ben's offer to settle for bright prospects in selling, he wonders whether he took the wrong course. More and more Ben's idea of the quick, decisive act, leading to a fabulous fortune, will appeal to him and help him decide to kill himself for the insurance money.

TECHNIQUE

Willy's first question to Ben as to where he went wrong is based upon his heartsick reaction to his meeting with Howard. This leads into the flashback scene in which Ben apparently gave Willy a chance to go to Alaska, shortly before Biff's great Senior game.

IMPORTANT THEMES

COUNTRY VERSUS CITY

Willy would enjoy working with his sons out in the open in the Alaskan timberlands; there would be no installments to pay and a man could make a fortune using his hands. Yet, prodded by Linda, Willy also finds the city challenging. Great wealth is there, too, if only those seeking it are well liked, presumably like Willy and Biff.

IMPORTANCE OF BEING WELL LIKED

Linda says that Willy is well liked. As a result he will be happy and he will also get to be a partner in the firm. Willy picks up her argument. Great fortunes can be made if a man has good contacts who like him. Willy incorrectly reasons that Biff is popular and so has offers from universities. Biff has the offers because he is a football star. Willy also falsely believes that Biff will be well received when he enters the business world.

SYMBOLS

The wash links Linda's concern for her household duties and identifies her with the settled life of an ordinary urban family. What this represents is diametrically opposed to the restless, opportunistic, adventurous life offered by Ben.

Ben is always en route to make new deals and conquer new territories. He also, one suspects, may be leaving some dubious practice as far behind him as possible. He wants nothing to do with law courts, or the regulation they impose upon rugged individuals. The umbrella might seem strange equipment for such a fearless type. But he has been seen to use it as a weapon, aiming it at Biff's eye.

Dave Singleman is the individual, the success. The aging salesman is used to conjure up visions of a leisurely, profitable selling career, once the contacts have been firmly established.

ACT II, SCENE 4
SUMMARY

In this flashback scene, it is the day of Biff's big game. Bernard and Happy contend for the honor of carrying Biff's helmet. If Biff wins, he will be captain of the championship city team. Charley teases Willy, who is feverishly enthusiastic, about never growing up. Willy, furious, blasts him for his ignorance.

CHARACTER ANALYSES

WILLY

Enormously proud of his football-hero son, Willy is boyishly eager to get to the field and wave his pennant. If this is Biff's greatest day, it is Willy's too. He is incredulous that Charley can be so stupid as to see it as only one more game and Willy as amusingly immature. Hot-tempered throughout his life, he wants to fight Charley but contents himself with name-calling. Although he sees the game as representing personal glory for Biff, as well as for his family, he also never loses sight of possible material rewards. Previously he has often mentioned the scholarship offers. Now he suggests that some professional team may pay Biff twenty-five thousand a year, the sum paid Red Grange. This shows that Willy has muddled ideas of success.

BIFF

In his few speeches, Biff is first of all eager to get started. He is also the lordly but gracious idol, as he kindly permits Bernard to carry his shoulder guards. Finally, he is Willy's devoted son, again promising to make a special touchdown just for Dad. This reveals that he is not a team player, foreshadowing his failure in business.

HAPPY AND BERNARD

Here, both characters are Biff's satellites, vying to carry his helmet and shoulder guards and be seen with him in the clubhouse. Both are pleased just to be part of his retinue.

CHARLEY

Here, Charley teases Willy unmercifully. Linda is probably right in her assertion that he is joking when he indicates that he did not know this was the day of the big game. Charley clearly considers football—indeed, all organized sports—only a boy's game, not worth all the fuss Willy makes over it. He is amusedly skeptical when Willy calls this the "greatest day" in Biff's life. Partly, then, Charley's jests stem from his own wry sense of humor, partly from the fact that his values differ markedly from Willy's.

PLOT DEVELOPMENT

Biff's sense of exaltation based on popularity and athletic prowess will be painfully lost when suddenly thereafter he is just one more student who failed a subject. The consequences of his fall will eventually lead to Willy's self-destruction. In addition, Willy's memory of his denunciation of Charley's stupidity is one more disturbing thought as he now, penniless after losing his job, comes to seek a "loan" from the still amicable, reasonably successful Charley.

TECHNIQUE

For this flashback scene there is the bright, cheerful music of happier times. In addition, it may be noted that when Willy goes from kitchen to living room, he seemingly walks through a wall. This practice, followed in other scenes taking place now in Willy's mind, increases the effect of a sort of dream vision.

IMPORTANT THEMES

IMPORTANCE OF ATHLETIC PROWESS

As champion, Biff will be cheered by thousands. His victory will mean that this is "the greatest day" of his life and may earn him a contract to be paid a great sum in professional football. Willy holds this value above academic achievement— the achievement that enabled Bernard to become a success.

FAMILY SOLIDARITY

All the Lomans are off to the game, one to play, the other three to cheer. Biff, in turn, promises to make a special touchdown for his father. This shows the family sticking together.

ACT II, SCENE 5
SUMMARY

It is the present. Willy walks into Charley's office and alarms Jenny, the secretary, with his wild mumbling. Then he tries to smooth over the situation with a feeble joke or two. He then meets Bernard, now an extremely prosperous young lawyer off to plead a case before the Supreme Court. Bernard takes tennis rackets to play on the courts of rich friends with whom he will stay. He is married and has two sons. Willy tries to bluff about Biff's success, but finally asks Bernard why Biff lost heart. Bernard cautiously suggests that Biff's collapse really occurred not after the school failure but following a subsequent visit to Willy in Boston. After that Biff fought Bernard and burned his prized sneakers. Disturbed by Bernard's hint that he was to blame, Willy turns on him furiously.

CHARACTER ANALYSES

WILLY

Several traits of Willy appear in this brief scene. First of all he is the disturbed personality, muttering something about touchdowns so that Jenny calls for help from Bernard. Then, getting hold of himself, he is again the genial salesman with a snappy quip for a pretty receptionist. Bernard's evident affluence much impresses him. To Willy, material possessions are extremely significant. If Bernard's friends own tennis courts, they must be "fine people." Bernard, having done so well, is no longer the anemic pest, but a "brilliant man." Willy as braggart is also here, for at first he tries almost pitiably to claim an equal success for Biff in the West. But soon he is again the forlorn, bewildered father, trying to understand. At the same time, he is not ready to accept any imputation of guilt, however blameworthy he actually feels. So once more his fiery temper flares.

BERNARD

Quietly assured, Bernard greets "Uncle Willy" pleasantly and asks about Biff. Generally tactful, he refrains from critical comments but tries to answer Willy's questions. In his account of Biff's erratic actions the summer after senior year, he reveals his love for Biff, despite the latter's having rarely treated him fairly. He does not know what happened in Boston but has realized that the incident there was crucial as far as Biff's later instability was concerned.

BIFF

From Bernard's account, young Biff was destroyed by what happened with Willy in Boston, although we do not yet know what it was that occurred. Biff pummeled the inoffensive Bernard and burned his sneakers, with the University's name printed on them, as an indication that he and abandoned all his high hopes.

PLOT DEVELOPMENT

In this present-day scene, Bernard's obvious prosperity and settled home life with a wife and two sons make Willy even more painfully aware of Biff's unproductive existence. This adds to his desperation. In addition, Bernard's account of the past stirs up guilt feelings that he has apparently been trying to suppress. Soon, however, the Boston episode will be uppermost in his mind, and this agonizing memory also will serve to impel him toward destruction.

TECHNIQUE

This scene is played on the front of the stage to the right. The office is suggested by a receptionist's small table. Bernard's suitcase and tennis rackets are props, and the lighting directs audience attention to this stage area.

IMPORTANT THEMES

"LOSTNESS"
Willy reveals to Bernard that he does not understand how so much could go wrong for Biff and begs for enlightenment.

FAMILY SOLIDARITY
Willy still wants to help Biff, his one lament being that he has "nothing to give him."

QUESTIONABLE MORALITY
At first Willy tries his usual lies, asserting that Biff is doing well out West and has actually been sent for by Oliver. Again, in talking of the teacher who failed Biff, Willy regards this action as evidence that the instructor was meanly responsible for ruining his son. For his part, while he talks of possibly having been at fault, Willy angrily denies being to blame once the idea has been broached by Bernard.

SYMBOLS
To Willy, the tennis rackets suggest the good, leisured society to which the fortunate Bernard has access.

The sneakers, as before, signify Biff's ambition to go on scholarship to the University. Burning them, he renounces his dream.

ACT II, SCENE 6
SUMMARY

Bernard leaves with a bottle of bourbon, a gift from Charley. Bidding Willy goodbye, he suggests that Willy "walk away" from the insoluble problem. Willy cannot. Willy is further startled to learn that Bernard will plead before the Supreme Court, although his father never lavished much attention on him. Charley again offers Willy a job but Willy furiously repulses him. Charley tells Willy to grow up and stop thinking about being well liked. Giving Willy the money he needs, he accuses him of being jealous. Thinking of his insurance, Willy says he is worth more dead. He leaves dreamily, sending apologies to Bernard and touchingly taking leave of Charley as his one and only friend.

CHARACTER ANALYSES

WILLY

Here certain contradictions in Willy's nature become even more obvious. He can steadily borrow from Charley sizable sums that he may never be able to repay. Yet because he is allegedly keeping strict accounts, he feels that he is not accepting favors. If Charley objects, he will walk out haughtily. When, however, Charley offers him a job with no traveling, paying as much as he begged from Howard, he refuses with finality. At first he says that he does not need a job, then he simply says that he cannot work for his friend. Becoming an employee of the "big ignoramus" he has always scorned would be an insupportable humiliation, whereas he can still apparently convince himself that he will pay back the "loans." Willy is a proud man and as irascible as ever. Yet his last word to Charley indicates that deep within him there is some sense of gratitude.

CHARLEY

Proud of Bernard, Charley implies that he succeeded as a father because he did not smother his son with attention the way Willy did Biff. He now sends Bernard off to Washington with a friendly wave and a man-to-man gift of bourbon. Still spirited enough to fend off Willy's worst insults, Charley compassionately offers his old antagonist a job. Yet he takes issue with Willy's insistence upon being well liked. Salesmen, he says, sell products, not themselves, and successful men are not always the most lovable types. Charley is also sharp enough to see that Willy is toying with the idea of suicide. He tries to dissuade him but Willy hardly listens. All in all, Charley stands for sensible action rather than big talk.

PLOT DEVELOPMENT

In refusing Charley's job offer, Willy proudly cuts off a final chance to maintain some self-respect as a wage-earner. In addition, in spite of himself, Charley's suggestion that his theory of being well liked is false reduces his self-assurance still further. Finally, Charley's mention of the insurance premium turns his thoughts to suicide, even though he still hopes that Biff may have succeeded.

TECHNIQUE

This is played in the same stage area as the preceding scene.

IMPORTANT THEMES

IMPORTANCE OF BEING WELL LIKED

Charley denies Willy's idea that being popular is the key to success.

CORRUPTION OF MODERN BUSINESS

Willy has harsh things to say about Howard. Charley, however, is a good, humane businessman and yet disputes Willy's claim that personal associations count for much. In apparent contradiction, however, he offers his broken friend a job.

SYMBOLS

The bottle of bourbon, a gift from Charley to his son Bernard, suggests a pleasant, friendly relationship between the two men. It points up their easy-going camaraderie as opposed to the tense, strained feelings between Willy and Biff, both of whom are in difficult economic positions.

ACT II, SCENE 7
SUMMARY

Awaiting Biff and Willy for dinner at the restaurant, Happy impresses the waiter, Stanley, with his sophisticated manner. Then he suavely picks up an attractive young diner, Miss Forsythe, bragging about himself and his brother. She leaves to find a friend for Biff, who has just arrived. Biff, much upset, says that after his long wait Oliver failed to recognize him. He was, after all, never a salesman, just a clerk. Impulsively, Biff stole Oliver's pen and ran away. He wants to tell Willy that he now realizes his limitations, but Happy warns him not to ruin Willy's hopes.

CHARACTER ANALYSES

HAPPY

This is Happy's scene. He shows a certain practiced deftness and savoir-faire in dealing with the waiter and the young prostitute, but he lies continually. There is also something cheap and second-rate in his pretensions to urbanity. He does, however, seem to be genuinely fond of his brother, and he is not without some consideration for Willy when he urges Biff not to tell him the worst. Of course, seeking the companionship of the two women when he and Biff had asked Willy to dinner shows a great deal of thoughtlessness, but Happy has long concentrated upon sexual affairs.

BIFF

Biff's theft of Oliver's pen recalls Biff's earlier stealing. But for all his disappointment, Biff here shows signs of growing up, of facing facts honestly. Yet in his eagerness to impart his new knowledge to Willy, thus clearing up any misapprehensions the older man may possess, he does not seem to consider at all the effect this might have upon Willy's distracted mental state.

PLOT DEVELOPMENT

Biff's determination to tell Willy how insignificant the Oliver interview made him feel will prove highly disturbing to his already desperate father. The date with the two women will provide the two sons with a tempting escape when Willy's erratic actions prove embarrassing.

TECHNIQUE

The restaurant scene, also played on the front part of the stage, is suggested by a reddish light, brassy orchestra, and the table and chairs the waiter and Happy bring out.

IMPORTANT THEMES

QUESTIONABLE MORALITY

Happy boasts about his brother as a big cattleman and a professional football star. He also tells of his mythical stay at West Point. He urges Biff to go on lying to their father. Biff, of course, has stolen again, but now he wants to admit the truth about himself.

CORRUPTION OF MODERN BUSINESS

The waiter is pleased to hear from Happy that the latter plans to go into business with his brother. In this place the bartender is always stealing from the boss.

FAMILY SOLIDARITY

Happy gets Biff a date, praising him highly. Happy tries to keep Willy happily anticipating Biff's success, while Biff thinks he will be better if he sees that Biff has failed from his own limitations and not merely to spite his father.

STEALING

Biff has taken Oliver's fountain pen. This time, however, he does not pass off his action lightly. He is horrified and ashamed.

SYMBOLS

Happy makes much of his "overseas" champagne cocktail recipe, and sends the woman champagne to start up an acquaintance. This is obviously a proof of Happy's Continental elegance and one of his symbols of sophistication.

Oliver's personal pen is the sign of his executive status, something used to sign important documents. After a long wait, Biff has been humiliatingly ignored. Taking the pen, a status symbol, is apparently almost an instinctive way of compensating for his injured pride. But the very irrationality of the act also helps to rouse Biff to realize the lie he has long been living.

ACT II, SCENE 8
SUMMARY

Willy joins his sons and the women and they order drinks. Already mildly intoxicated, Biff tries to tell Willy the grim facts, but both boys are shocked to hear that Willy has lost his job. From then on, Willy goes on assuming that Oliver welcomed Biff, and Happy encourages this delusion. Biff wavers between keeping Willy cheerful and admitting the dismal truth. Finally, Willy gets angry, and Biff gives up.

CHARACTER ANALYSES

WILLY

Bereft of all hopes and anxious to bring Linda back some good news, Willy wants only reassuring words from Biff, and therefore he angrily berates his son whenever he tries to give an honest account. Willy always was enough of an optimist to make the most of the slightest encouraging sign, but here his own despair makes him try to find reason for rejoicing where none whatsoever exists. Because he is attempting the impossible, his temper is soon out of control, and he becomes increasingly harder to soothe.

BIFF

Anxious to reveal the new truths he has painfully discovered, Biff is also distressed to see his father so depressed and distraught. In addition, he is used to having his mind made up for him by the strong-willed older man. Thus he finds it hard to speak his piece. Furthermore, feeling the effects of what he has been drinking, he is not altogether in a reasonable frame of mind. So as Willy continues to bait him, he finally gives up trying.

HAPPY

Happy's one concern is to calm Willy down. With this in mind, he lies continually, regardless of what Biff says, to let Willy go on thinking that Biff favorably impressed Oliver.

PLOT DEVELOPMENT

Willy's last hope has now been shattered. Excited and irritable, he will become hopelessly unmanageable and thus make impossible what was to have been a pleasant dinner party with his sons.

TECHNIQUE

This is a straight present-day scene played at the front of the stage as was the previous one.

IMPORTANT THEMES

IMPORTANCE OF BEING WELL LIKED

Willy is certain that Oliver must have remembered Biff, because he has deluded himself into thinking that Biff formerly had impressed him. Just the opposite is true.

FAMILY SOLIDARITY

Willy wants good news so that Linda will suffer less. The boys are sorry for him and want to calm him. Biff favors telling him the truth; Happy leans toward the reassuring lie.

QUESTIONABLE MORALITY

Willy does not want to hear that Biff was a mere shipping clerk rather than a salesman. Happy lies repeatedly about the Oliver interview.

SYMBOL

Willy uses the image of the burning woods to distinguish between the threatening total catastrophe and mere minor setbacks. The woods represent total catastrophe.

ACT II, SCENE 9
SUMMARY

As Biff talks, Willy, distracted, hears young Bernard announcing to Linda that Biff failed mathematics and has gone to Boston to see Willy. The present-day Biff, bewildered by his father's talk of the old math failure, tries to tell him about the fountain pen. Willy slips back into his Boston memory. He is being paged in a hotel and his woman companion urges him to open the door. Meanwhile, Biff has been unable to make Willy see why he cannot return to talk again to Oliver. Finally, the girls return, and Willy staggers off to the men's room. Unable to cope with him further, Biff leaves, imploring Happy to stay. Happy, however, disowns his father and follows Biff with the two prostitutes after paying the bill.

CHARACTER ANALYSES

WILLY

In relatively lucid moments, Willy tries to coach Biff on how to lie to Oliver about having gone off with his pen. He does everything possible to avoid facing facts, and when he can no longer do so, he bitterly denounces Biff. Actually, however, in this scene he is becoming increasingly distraught, since he keeps drifting back to the Boston episode in the past.

BIFF

Confused by Willy's references to events long ago, Biff still tries to explain why he cannot again approach Oliver. Yet as Willy eyes him accusingly, Biff seems the small boy again denying that he intended to steal at all. Afterwards, alarmed at Willy's condition, Biff resorts again to less disturbing lies but he still wants to tell Willy the truth. Eventually, unable to stand the tensions and having been struck and called names by Willy, Biff goes off. Before leaving, however, he tells the women that Willy is really a prince.

HAPPY

Before going, Biff asks Happy to look after Willy. When the younger son demurs, Biff accuses him of not caring for their father. Happy is angered, with some justice, for he has at least made some attempts to help Willy. Yet a moment later, he goes off with the women and even denies that Willy is his father at all. In general, he is colder than Biff. Whereas the older brother flees in agony, Happy is off to salvage a good time. Essentially, however, both reveal their cowardice in so deserting the disagreeable but sadly disturbed Willy.

PLOT DEVELOPMENT

As his despair increases through Biff's revelations, Willy becomes more and more upset. His mind recalls the unhappy past when Biff failed and the Boston episode wrecked their happy relationship. Obviously, being deserted now by his sons will do nothing to restore his emotional balance.

TECHNIQUE

This is a complicated scene technically. A soft, misty light comes up on the house as young Bernard announces Biff's failure to Linda. A trumpet note indicates that Willy has a sudden, sharp recollection. "Hearing" young Bernard's announcement, Willy in the present abuses the older Biff. Again, as they argue further, the laughter of the Boston woman is heard from the left of the stage. Willy talks sometimes to the Boston telephone operator, sometimes to the woman, sometimes to the present-day Biff.

IMPORTANT THEMES

FATHER-SON CONFLICT

When Biff tries to tell Willy the truth, Willy accuses him of spiting him and of being nothing but a "rotten little louse." Biff tries to calm him and even to see him as he used to appear to him a "pal," or a "good companion." But the relationship is now merely a torment. So Biff leaves.

QUESTIONABLE MORALITY

Willy insists that Biff lie to Oliver about taking the pen. Happy tells the girls that Willy is not his father. Biff and Happy both walk away from the disturbed Willy, who was their invited guest.

SYMBOL

Before leaving, Biff takes out the tubing and shows it to Happy. He asks Happy to stop Willy from killing himself, but Happy refuses the assignment while not denying that such is Willy's intent.

ACT II, SCENE 10
SUMMARY

In this flashback, Willy is sharing a hotel room with the Boston woman, Miss Francis. Someone keeps knocking on the door. Finally, Willy sends Miss Francis into the bathroom and opens the door. Biff is at the door. He has come to confess his failure and beg Willy to talk to his teacher, Mr. Birnbaum. He admits having missed the class and made fun of his teacher. The woman comes in, to Biff's horror, and Willy tries to invent a plausible explanation. The woman leaves but first demands her promised gift of stockings. Biff sobs, and Willy tries desperately to win him over, insisting that he was lonely and that the woman did not mean anything to him. Biff, however, calls him a liar and a fake and says he does not want to go to the University.

Back in the present, Stanley, the waiter, tells Willy that his sons have left. Willy tips him too lavishly and oddly sets out to buy seeds.

CHARACTER ANALYSES

WILLY

Even before Biff arrives, Willy is uneasy in the hotel. The knocking unnerves him, and the woman describes him as unhappy and selfish. Unexpectedly encountering Biff, he tries to bluff his way out of an embarrassing situation and all but throws the woman out. When all else fails, he resorts to the truth, but by then Biff is sadly disillusioned. As for Biff's failure, it is significant that Willy at this point does not blame Biff. In fact, he enjoys his account of how he mockingly imitated the teacher's lisp and is annoyed that Bernard did not furnish enough answers. His love for Biff is apparent throughout, but his behavior gives the boy some cause to consider him a liar.

BIFF

Young Biff first shows here a childish faith that his father can

talk the teacher into giving him the points he needs to graduate. The minute he has trouble, he runs off to get help from
Dad. His thinking, too, is immature: he failed the course
because the teacher hated him, not because he did not do the
work. When afterwards Biff discovers his father's liaison, he
bursts into angry tears, will listen to no explanation, and calls
his fallen idol names. He is particularly distressed that Willy
has given the buyer "Mama's stockings." Now that his faith
has been shattered, he will do nothing about summer school
and does not want to go to the University at all. There is
heartbreak and disillusionment here, but Biff seems to react
like a small child, rather than a young man of college age.
Willy has, of course, always played the hero in front of Biff.
Now Biff passionately denounces him as a fraud.

PLOT DEVELOPMENT

From Biff's first references in Act I to Willy as a "fake," an
explanation has been forthcoming. Bernard's references to
Boston and his question about what happened there com-
pounded the suspense. This scene explains the tensions
between Willy and Biff and suggests why Biff never went on
to succeed when he seemed to have such bright prospects.
As a memory it involves deep feelings of guilt on Willy's part,
and his reliving it at this time increases his sense of being lost.
Some commentators have doubted that the revelation of Willy's
extramarital affair could really have had such a cataclysmic
effect on a normally resilient young man. Others justify this as
plausible on the grounds that Willy's dubious "training" had
given Biff no adequate preparation for coping with the reali-
ties of a far from perfect world. Discovering Willy's betrayal
was probably the bitterest possible blow that Biff could have
received.

TECHNIQUE

The sensual aspect of Willy's affair is suggested by the type of
sexy background music being played. The scene is played at
the front of the stage, and lighting is used to pick out the

principal figures. There is otherwise no hotel-room set or furnishings.

IMPORTANT THEMES

FATHER-SON CONFLICT

Willy has done nothing directly to injure Biff. He wants only to help his son get to college, but Biff has had his illusions wrecked and is both miserable and furious. The moment before, he was blithely confident that Dad could fix anything, even a failing mark. From now on, however, the idyll is over. Biff and Willy will quarrel heatedly, be partially reconciled, then quarrel again.

THE IMPORTANCE OF BEING WELL LIKED

Biff assures Willy that if he talks to Birmbaum in his impressive fashion, the teacher will alter the grade. Willy, for his part, is flattered by his son's admiration. He also enjoys hearing how Biff mimicked the teacher to the great delight of his admiring classmates.

QUESTIONABLE MORALITY

Biff has no compunction about having missed classes or cheated on exams. He is only sorry that he let his father down. Willy is annoyed that Bernard did not cheat more efficiently so that Biff could have passed. Willy lies to Biff about the woman in his room, and finally excuses his actions on the grounds that he was lonely.

SYMBOLS

Throughout the play Willy has been uneasy whenever he sees Linda darning old stockings. The stockings he gives Miss Francis are partially a business investment, for she can get him in to see buyers. They also make Willy a generous, desirable man to know and thus make him feel like the "big shot" he wants to be. To Biff, however, they represent an insult to his mother and they thus increase his bitterness regarding Willy's deception.

Willy asks the waiter where he can buy seeds. He wants something to grow in his garden. He has just been deserted by his sons, and in a sense they were his plants, his future growth. Now he will try once more to raise vegetables from the ground, so that something will grow and flourish.

ACT II, SCENE 11
SUMMARY

Arriving home late with roses as a peace offering, the boys are met by a bitterly indignant Linda. Throwing down the flowers, she denounces the pair for deserting their father and tells both to pack and leave. Happy tries lying to gloss over the situation. Biff is remorseful and contrite. He begs to see his father before he goes. Willy, however, is out planting vegetables.

CHARACTER ANALYSES

LINDA

Unyielding, almost ferocious in her denunciation of her sons, Linda will listen to no excuses. Willy is her one concern. She is more wife than mother, although she sometimes seems to mother Willy. Seemingly meek and uncomplaining whenever her husband speaks, she is here hard, relentless, even somewhat coarse. Only when she suddenly fears that she cannot by strong words stop Biff from harassing Willy further, does she adopt a milder tone and actually beg. Some critics have wondered whether or not such a positive, uncompromising woman would be likely to take so much verbal abuse from the moody Willy. Is it just that she loves him more than she does her sons? It may be noted, of course, that even though she talks soothingly to Willy, she keeps close accounts of the finances and does tend to run his life. It was she who did battle with Ben, and it was she who promoted the meeting with Howard.

HAPPY

A little afraid of his irate mother, Happy tries as usual to lie his way out of difficulties. His assurance that Willy actually had a good time with them is obviously implausible, for Willy has come home before them. But Happy is forever trying to keep others satisfied by making free with the facts. When his lies fail to convince, he goes upstairs without apology.

BIFF

As opposed to his callous brother, Biff is conscience-stricken. He does try to tell Linda that Willy is not yet dying, but he makes no serious effort to defend his own actions. He also rudely cuts off Happy's attempts to suggest that Willy did have a pleasant evening. Humbled and remorseful, Biff still insists upon seeing Willy and Linda is forced to recognize that Biff, too, can on occasion be a determined individual.

PLOT DEVELOPMENT

Linda's ultimatum that the boys must leave will hasten the crucial scene between Biff and Willy that will lead to the latter's suicide. The scene also reveals vital differences in the personalities of the two sons. Morally, there is some hope for Biff, little for Happy.

TECHNIQUE

This scene is played in the kitchen and living room of the house. Lighting is used effectively, especially when the fearful boys discover that Linda knows what has happened and she moves toward them furiously.

IMPORTANT THEMES

FAMILY SOLIDARITY

Linda has no qualms about insisting that the boys take responsibility for Willy. Since Willy is not well and was their guest, she is obviously justified here. But, throughout, this emphasis upon obligations of parent to grown son and grown son to parent is quite pronounced. Charley and Bernard talk of letting things go and walking away. The Lomans cannot seem to accept this.

QUESTIONABLE MORALITY

Linda denounces the desertion of Willy as cruel and inhuman. Happy goes on lying to make Linda less angry and to make things easier for him and Biff. Linda also has harsh words for their dealing with the two prostitutes, although Happy assures her, probably truthfully for once, that all he and the women did was follow the morose Biff and try to cheer him up.

SYMBOLS

Ordinarily, Linda would probably welcome the roses—an attractive, fairly expensive present—but here she roughly pushes them out of Happy's hands. As she declared in the beginning, she will not remain on friendly terms with anyone who is unkind to Willy. In rejecting the roses, she is rejecting her sons because of their having hurt her husband.

Like the seeds, in the previous scene, the garden is Willy's pathetic attempt to start something for the future. When Ben offered him the Alaska post, he told him he was building his fortune through his sales work. He also looked to Biff to carry on the Loman name with distinction. Now both of these hopes have faded. So in the dead of night he is out planting vegetables.

ACT II, SCENE 12
SUMMARY

Busy planting carrots and lettuce by flashlight, Willy starts consulting a vision of Ben about killing himself for his twenty-thousand-dollar insurance money. Ben admits that this is a substantial sum but wonders about the certainty of payment and about Willy's being called a coward. Willy, however, sees his suicide as giving Biff a "diamond." Biff would also be impressed by Willy's funeral, with mourners from distant states. But Ben frightens him by suggesting that Biff might only hate him.

CHARACTER ANALYSES

WILLY

Here Willy, gardening in the dark, is hardly rational. He is obsessed with the idea of leaving a great sum to Biff. Presumably if Biff sees that his father is able to give him such a sum, then Biff will stop spiting Willy and make a success of his life. Then Willy will be assured of a sort of immortality. Willy thinks of Ben in connection with this insurance project because it involves a large fortune made instantaneously—a found "diamond," not small sums made through endless appointments. Ben also would not be one to show overconcern about the morality of the proposition. Yet even considering the act in practical terms, Willy is not sure how Biff will judge him. He does not merely want Biff to have the money; he also wants Biff to honor his memory. So in considering the possibility of committing suicide, Willy wants to be able to leave something to Biff as well as the long-suffering Linda. But he is also, as the Boston woman long ago suggested, "self-centered" enough to want proper recognition for the sacrifice of his life. As for the morality of suicide, or of cheating insurance companies, Willy is not concerned.

Willy has a child's view of what is fair and unfair. He has had to work hard over the years to pay his premiums. He believes that the least the company can do is pay him if he's willing to kill himself for money.

BEN

In earlier scenes Willy's memories may or may not represent the older brother, Ben, as he actually was in life. Here Ben is clearly an imaginary being. In the debate over suicide, he is actually that side of Willy's personality that has always admired swift, decisive action and looked for wealth to be obtained in an audacious coup. In addition, "Ben" always seems to personify a certain lawlessness, an impatience with the stricter requirements of ethics. Willy has never been overly scrupulous about the property of others. "Ben" also stands for a combination of selfishness and hard-headed practicality. This type of mind can appreciate material wealth in the form of diamonds or cash in lump sums, but it is skeptical about building a business through friendly contacts or counting upon a son's admiration for a suicide father. As both a materialist and a man of action, the "Ben" side finds self-destruction a negative course and is cynical enough to wonder whether or not it would pay off at all. Speaking in his own person, Willy has some generous concern for Linda and Biff, as well as an egotistic urge to prove that he is known to many. Yet it is the adventurous, opportunistic "Ben" in him that prompts him to a final desperate undertaking.

PLOT DEVELOPMENT

Suicide has been hinted at previously. Linda has spoken of Willy's other attempts to the boys; Biff has found the rubber tubing; and Charley has noted Willy's reference to his being worth more dead than alive. Here, however, the plan is seen actually taking form. Willy's death thus seems imminent. Yet for the moment, his worries about Biff's possible reaction postpone the move. The very fact, of course, that Willy is conversing with a long-dead brother and not merely remembering indicates considerable mental disturbance.

TECHNIQUE

This scene takes place in the garden on the apron or front part of the stage. A soft blue light suggests night. Willy uses a flashlight to read the directions on his seed packets and occasionally uses a hoe. Ben appears out of the darkness to the right. This is the first time that Willy holds a discussion with a figure from his past. Hitherto he has apparently just relived crucial experiences, although sometimes commenting upon them in a manner that confuses present-day characters, as when he talks to the grown Biff about failing in school.

IMPORTANT THEMES

FAMILY SOLIDARITY

Willy can talk only to his brother Ben. He wants to kill himself so that Linda and Biff will have what he can give them.

THE IMPORTANCE OF BEING WELL LIKED

Willy feels that Biff will be impressed to see how well known Willy was, when all the old friends who liked him came from New England and elsewhere to attend his funeral. Willy is again engaging in grandiose visions. In fact, only his family and the two neighbors will come to the funeral.

QUESTIONABLE MORALITY

Willy seems unconcerned about the moral aspects of taking one's own life. To him it is not cowardly, yet he would not want to have Biff think him a coward or a fool. He also has no worries about whether or not he may be guilty of fraud as far as the insurance claim is concerned.

LAMENT FOR THE PAST

Willy poignantly recalls the days when the healthy young Biff used to enjoy winter sports and carry his sample cases and polish the car. How, he asks, can one recover such peaks of happiness?

SYMBOLS

As before, Willy's absurd planting operation represents his desperate urge to accomplish something, to build a future for his heirs.

Throughout the play, the diamonds have been Willy's symbol for great, satisfying wealth—beautiful and impressive. Here he equates his diamond with money the insurance company will pay his family if he kills himself. It would prove him a man worth respecting, and it would be a dazzlingly large lump sum, not little amounts pieced together by endless selling appointments.

ACT II, SCENE 13
SUMMARY

Biff joins Willy in the garden and tells him he is leaving for good. Uneasy about facing Linda and furious that Biff will not try to see Oliver again, Willy refuses a good-bye handshake. He curses Biff for spiting him. Stung, Biff takes out the rubber tube and calls Willy a fake. As Linda and Happy watch helpless, Biff admits that he was in jail in Kansas City for stealing a suit. He has always stolen because Willy made him think he must be important, but without exerting the effort. He is through running. He will go back to the West, to the work he likes. Both he and his father must face it that they are not leaders. Willy denies this irately, but Biff, no longer angry, sobs brokenly. All he asks is that Willy burn his false dreams.

CHARACTER ANALYSES

WILLY

Willy is roused to fury and bitterness by his sense of guilt. If Biff is failing, Biff must be still taking revenge for the Boston disillusionment because if Biff is not failing deliberately, then Willy is to blame, and that sort of burden Willy cannot shoulder. If, however, Biff has become a drifter out of spite, then Willy, however outraged by such ingratitude and meanness, can judge himself blameless. One lapse on his part obviously did not deserve such a long campaign of calculated insult and retribution. Biff offers a third explanation, that he never possessed the extraordinary potential Willy attributed to him and hence would under no circumstances have been a great leader. Willy finds this explanation almost equally obnoxious. For if Biff does not succeed magnificently, then Biff is nothing. And if Biff is nothing, so is Willy. And Willy has spent a lifetime covering up the discouraging smallness of his income by picturing himself as a dynamic, aggressive salesman universally admired. As the heir apparent, Biff could easily surpass even his father's enviable record. If Willy accepts Biff's less flattering appraisal of both of them, then he must not only give up the emotional props he has relied on over the years. He must also admit that even if his Boston affair did not wreck Biff, the way he "trained" his son, of which he was so proud, left his son inadequately prepared for life. This idea, again demanding an admission of guilt, is equally insupportable. So Willy, with no job and no future, and fearful of losing all remaining shreds of self-esteem, shouts imprecations at the relentless Biff. Biff may hope to stave off Willy's suicide by making his father come to terms with reality. Willy, however, recoils with horror and fury when Biff attacks his foolish illusions.

BIFF

Highly emotional throughout this climactic scene, Biff first tries to take leave of Willy amicably, thus putting an end to the quarrels that are causing both of them such agony. As Willy, however, not only refuses a parting blessing but angrily denounces Biff as spiteful, the younger man becomes irate in turn and insists upon destroying Willy's false picture of both of them once and for all. The more Willy tries to shy away from unpleasant truths, the more the now remorseless Biff tries to force them upon him. Biff starts by denying that he has any wish to blame Willy. But once roused by Willy's accusations of spite, he indicates that he sees that his repeated thefts, culminating in a jail term, are traceable to Willy's having created in him a false impression that he was never meant to be a subordinate, but always an executive. While he is at it, Biff also points out that Happy is not an assistant buyer as he claims but only one of those helping the assistant buyer.

In this scene Biff does show some progress toward maturity. He no longer has quite so unrealistic a picture of his own capabilities as he had. He says that he is through with stealing, and he also has recognized the kind of outdoor life he wants and will pursue it presumably without making impossible demands of it. At the same time, he still reveals some traits that do not suggest an adult personality. For one thing, he is not in command of his emotions. At one moment he is ready to strike Willy, and shortly thereafter he breaks down and sobs. Secondly, he is all too ready to shunt the blame for his own criminal acts onto Willy. Biff claims that it was Willy's fault that he stole. Finally, he tends to go to extremes. He and Willy may not be the extraordinary people Willy always envisioned, but whether they are a "dime a dozen," or even "nothing," is debatable.

PLOT DEVELOPMENT

Willy has regarded his projected suicide as a grand gesture that will marvelously impress Biff. But in taking out the rubber tube and flinging it at Willy, Biff denies that he will regard Willy as any hero at all. Taken with the doubts expressed by "Ben," this would seem to be a deterrent. In this scene, Biff also tries to make Willy give up his self-important delusions. There is no indication that he succeeds. Willy may still go ahead with his plan. Linda and Happy seem increasingly unable to influence either Biff or Willy.

TECHNIQUE

Played partially out on the stage apron (the garden), the scene moves into the kitchen. There are no flashbacks. In terms of dramatic structure, this is a great "confrontation scene," in which two antagonists face each other and take up some vital issue to settle once and for all. It might also be termed a "necessary scene." There has been much in the play about the relationship between Willy and Biff, and Biff has been reticent about the causes of his hostility. Here we learn some of his feelings, that the play has been promising all along.

IMPORTANT THEMES

FATHER-SON CONFLICT

Willy tries to blame Biff for spitefully refusing to succeed. Biff claims that Willy's false teaching encouraged him to steal and also to be confused about his true nature. He also calls his father a fake for toying with the idea of suicide.

QUESTIONABLE MORALITY

Biff reveals that he served a three-month jail term for stealing a suit. He blames Willy for having given him false teaching. He accuses Happy of lying and says that in the Loman house, no one ever told the truth.

SYMBOLS

To Biff, the rubber tube proves Willy a fraud and no hero. If Willy kills himself, Biff will have no pity for him.

Representing to Biff the life of a business executive, Oliver's pen now seems to him the symbol of all that he wants to reject—the stealing and the running away, the whole business world. Instead, he is going back to the Western open-air work that he finds satisfying.

ACT II, SCENE 14
SUMMARY

Convinced by Biff's agonized sobs that his son loves him, Willy again sees Ben and thinks of the twenty thousand dollars. After promising his mother that he'll get married, Happy goes upstairs. Linda pleads with Willy to join her and also goes upstairs. After she goes, Willy talks to Ben about Biff's magnificence with all that money. Ben agrees that Willy would be fetching a diamond out of the jungle. Willy thinks once more of Biff's football glory and then after a momentary panic rushes off. After the musical suggestion of a crash, the family prepares for Willy's funeral.

CHARACTER ANALYSES

WILLY

Despite the harsh words uttered in fear and anger, Willy shows his deep love for Biff. He also still has his vision of Biff as magnificent and believes he will realize it by getting his son the insurance money. Willy also takes tender leave of Linda, sorry that she is so tired. He is hopeful now that everything will work out for the best. In carrying off the "proposition," he will have succeeded himself and made success possible for Biff, thus pulling victory out of defeat. He is fearful but triumphant. He is also not sane.

LINDA

Having made her peace with her sons, Linda fearfully suspects what Willy intends to do, yet she goes off and leaves the distracted man alone. The only preparation for this action has been her custom of leaving the rubber tubing where it was when Willy was home to help preserve his dignity. Linda does not want Willy to kill himself, but apparently cannot bring herself to interfere in order to stop him. There may be some question of plausibility here, but if Willy were determined enough, presumably he could kill himself sometime.

PLOT DEVELOPMENT

By an ironic twist, Biff's impassioned plea, intended to convince Willy that he is a "nothing," hence not worth the sacrifice of someone's life, has just the opposite effect. Suddenly certain of Biff's love, Willy sees his son as "magnificent," needing only wealth to far outdistance Bernard. Thus he is now convinced that suicide is the answer and receives confirmation from the vision of "Ben" that this is the way to get diamonds out of the jungle.

TECHNIQUE

Light and sound effects are used here to suggest first of all Willy's distraction and momentary panic. Then music conveys the idea of a car crash and subsequently makes the transition necessary to start the family toward Willy's funeral. The grave is located at the center front of the stage apron. Thus when the characters talk around the grave, they seem almost to be talking directly to the audience.

IMPORTANT THEMES

FAMILY SOLIDARITY

By his suicide, Willy will give Biff the chance for magnificence. Linda speaks encouragingly about both sons and indicates her love for Willy. As the funeral music starts, the family moves together, joined by Bernard and Charley.

IMPORTANCE OF PHYSICAL PROWESS

Willy last imagines Biff as the football hero. Biff's football is important and important people are watching him. Biff's skill at the game is still a vital element in his father's concept of his magnificence.

SYMBOLS

Ben keeps talking of taking diamonds out of the jungle. To Willy, the jungle seems to be the world in general that has made it hard for him to get ahead. The money he gets through his suicide will make jungle fighting easier for Biff. At the same time Willy has seen himself, as he remarked to Howard, as coming from a race of adventurous men with a streak of self-reliance. Such men—Ben included—tame jungles and are not tamed by them. And here Willy conquers his.

Again the insurance money is equated with diamonds. There is, first of all, a splendor about such stones, and Willy means his death to be a noble gesture. Secondly, they suggest great wealth, not small sums—and twenty thousand is more than Willy has ever had at one time. Finally, diamonds are made to represent a prize won by daring and initiative, by the bold stroke of an adventurous spirit. And this, too, is the way Willy regards the money he wants to leave Biff. Incidentally, the play never reveals whether or not Biff ever gets the money. It is never again mentioned.

REQUIEM

SUMMARY

Only Linda, her sons and Charley and Bernard join at Willy's grave. Linda laments that no one else came to the funeral. She cannot understand Willy's suicide at this time, when they were almost free of debt and their needs were small. Biff sadly remembers the good old days when they all repaired the house, but insists that Willy's dreams were wrong. Charley defends Willy as a true salesman "riding on a smile and a shoeshine." Biff, unconvinced, invites Happy to head West with him, but Happy is determined to realize Willy's dream in the city. Linda, kneeling, sorrowfully bids Willy farewell. Weeping, she goes off with Biff.

CHARACTER ANALYSES

LINDA

Here, Linda expresses the tender grief of one who had a deep love for Willy. Even if he was not a well-known or well-liked man, not a single business acquaintance comes to his funeral. Linda still believes that Willy was someone who was loved and missed. Her remarks to the effect that Willy's act is inexplicable because they were "free and clear" do not sound like those of the woman who was always ready to cite facts and figures and presumably knew that Willy had lost his job. From the first she knew about Willy's suicidal notions and earlier had offered some possible explanations to the boys. In terms of the drama, however, her expression of sorrow and loss is quite affecting.

BIFF

This scene shows that Biff has not changed his position. He can remember warmly and pleasurably the early days when he and his father and brother fixed the stoop and added a new porch, but sorrow over Willy's death has not altered his conviction that Willy's basic point of view was wrong. He is still, as he declared before, going back out West where he has been happiest. He even tries to coax Happy into going with him. As Charley's defense of Willy suggests, Biff is still perhaps too intolerant. Must Willy's dreams have been "all, all wrong?" But Biff at least has solved his own dilemma and can now go back to his ranch life, without feeling guilty because he is not making a name for himself in the urban business world that he so hates.

HAPPY

Not unaffected by his father's death, Happy still voices the old Loman dream "to come out number one." Yet his references to not being "licked," and to showing everybody in the "racket" suggest that eventually he, too, may be headed for disaster. Throughout the play, Happy has shown no inclination to work harder than ever or do his job more efficiently. All his talk has been of getting away with bribes and seducing other men's fiancées, of being slickly "covered" for unauthorized time off and of feeling nothing but contempt for those giving him orders. Even in the crucial scene of the showdown, he objected when Biff pointed out that he was only one of two assistants to the assistant buyer. Despite occasional pledges to get married, Happy does not seem to have changed at all. So his blithe assurances that he will "beat this racket" seem discouragingly hollow.

CHARLEY

In defending the man who always tended to insult him, Charley shows considerable understanding of the demands of a salesman's line of work. His line about "a smile and a shoeshine" is one of the most famous in the entire play. Throughout the play, Charley has been a sympathetic, helpful neighbor. Like Linda's tearful laments, Charley's words add sentiment and are appropriate to the kindly old friend. But essentially they only make one lament Willy's passing and brush aside whatever critical approach has hitherto been taken.

PLOT DEVELOPMENT

The plot virtually ends with Willy's suicide. Apart from the sad or elegiac tapering off here, however, this scene rounds out the story of Willy's sons. Happy will go on following Willy's impractical course. Biff, rejecting Willy's dream, will pursue his own objectives.

TECHNIQUE

As previously indicated, holding the requiem scene at the very front of the stage brings the audience into closer contact with those making final comments. The flute music at the end and the lighting that throws into relief the tall, almost menacing apartment buildings also add their own subtle interpretive effects.

IMPORTANT THEMES

IMPORTANCE OF PHYSICAL PROWESS

Biff happily remembers the work with their hands that gave the Loman men such satisfaction. Charley and Linda agree nostalgically that Willy was happy when manual skills were demanded.

FATHER-SON CONFLICT

Even though Willy is dead, Biff is still arguing with him. He condemns Willy's dreams at Willy's grave and tries to get his brother to give up the impossible struggle for impressive wealth and fame.

CORRUPTION OF MODERN BUSINESS

The terms in which Happy alludes to the city world—the "racket," in which he is going to show everybody that he can come out on top—recall all that has previously been said about the intense competition and low moral standards in business. By contrast, Biff's call to join him in the more easygoing West sounds like a last chance for health and sanity.

LAMENT FOR THE PAST

Biff affectionately remembers the old days when Willy and the boys worked happily together to fix up the house.

SYMBOLS

Linda, always the woman of the house, is particularly saddened to think that now that the mortgage has been finally paid off, Willy will not be there to share the building with her. In a sense, the house represents the whole of their thirty-five hard-working years together. Their marriage has been the struggle to possess a house. Biff, too, refers to parts of the house, such as stoop, cellar, and porch. To him they represent Willy's expert carpentering skills, and hence the answer to his unrealistic or wrong dreams. They also signify the good years of cooperative effort when family harmony prevailed.

ANALYSES OF MAJOR CHARACTERS

WILLY LOMAN

In a sense there are two Willy Lomans in this play. There is the present broken, exhausted man in his sixties, soon to end his life. There is also the more confident, vigorous Willy of some fifteen years before, who appears in the flashbacks. One actor portrays both, readily shifting from one representation to the other. To some extent, of course, the personality remains constant. The younger Willy, although given to boastful blustering, does admit misgivings to Linda and loneliness to Biff. The shattered older man, in turn, occasionally reverts to his former manner of jaunty optimism. Yet the changes are great and significant. The earlier Willy could never have been the idol of his teen-aged sons had he behaved in the perverse, distracted fashion of his older self.

Willy's agitation during his last days stems from a twofold sense of failure. He has not been able to launch his beloved son Biff successfully in the world, and he no longer can meet the demands of his own selling job. Although not altogether ignoring Linda and Happy, he is primarily concerned about the once magnificent young football star who at thirty-four drifts from one temporary ranch job to the next. Willy cannot "walk away" from Biff's problem, as Bernard suggests, nor can he accept Linda's view that "life is a casting off." Being over sixty, Willy is doubtless tiring physically. The sample cases are heavy. The seven-hundred-mile drives are arduous. Many business contacts, developed over the years, are vanishing as the men of his era die or retire. Yet the worry over Biff has obviously accelerated his collapse.

Willy's attitude toward Biff is complex. On the one hand, there is a strong personal attachment. He wants Biff to love him. He remembers yearningly the fondness Biff showed him as a boy, and he still craves this. At this point, however, relations are strained. Although Willy shies away from remembering so painful an episode, he knows in his heart that the Boston affair left the boy bitterly disillusioned. Feeling some sense of guilt, Willy fears that all of Biff's later difficulties may really have been attempts to get revenge. Biff has failed, in other words, mainly to "spite" Willy. Although outwardly resenting such alleged vindictiveness. Willy still wants to get back the old comradeship, even if he has to buy it dearly. "Why can't I give him something," he asks the spectral Ben, "and not have him hate me?" And his great final moment of joy and triumph occurs when he can exclaim, "Isn't that remarkable? Biff—he likes me!"

On the other hand, Willy is also emotionally involved with Biff because his son's success or failure is also his. By becoming rich and influential, the handsome, personable Biff was slated to provide Willy's victorious reply to all not sufficiently impressed with his own modest advancement. By making his fortune in the business world, Biff would prove that Willy had been right in turning down Ben's adventurous challenge to head for Alaska. He would also outshine sensible, hard working Charley and Bernard, thus establishing once and for all Willy's theory that having personality and being "well liked" were the great requisites for preeminence. Losing his own job, Willy is naturally unhappy, but if he can still purchase success for Biff with the insurance money, he personally will yet have won. "I always knew one way or another we were gonna make it, Biff and I!"

If Willy at any stage is apt to overindulge in grandiose daydreams, he is hardly the "phoney little fake" he seems to the shocked Biff. He works steadily at one job for thirty-six years and pays off a long-term mortgage, even if at the end he accepts some help from Charley. He takes good care of the house, too, capably making even major repairs. Although not altogether faithful, he is a reasonably satisfactory husband to Linda, who obviously respects him. He does not like to see her work too hard. When he loses his job, he is sorry to think how much she has suffered. In his own way, too, he has the makings of an admirable father. He gives much attention to his boys, showing them how to do things, working with them, and praising their accomplishments. He roots for them at their games, and defends them loyally. When Biff fails, Willy pays for several correspondence courses, even though he has to pawn his prized diamond watch fob given him by Ben. Finally, there is genuine dignity in the man when he spiritedly speaks up for his rights with Howard.

Willy is partially a victim of circumstance. He could not have avoided getting old and tired, any more than he could have prevented the building of the apartments that hem in his house. What's more, Willy did not originate some of the erroneous concepts and values that helped defeat him. The idea of the fast-made fortune, the "quick killing," is, to some extent, characteristically American. Our history certainly indicates that some people did reach the top by combining personal attractiveness with a casual disregard for ethical practice. Moreover, Willy was hardly the first in our society to overemphasize athletic prowess at the expense of steady intellectual work.

Yet in placing excessive reliance upon these dubious success formulas, Willy fails to take a realistic view of his limitations and those of his son. By all but encouraging Biff's petty thievery and giving it the flattering name of "initiative," he steers Biff toward an eventual jail term and Happy toward the discreditable habit of taking bribes. By running down the importance of good grades, he prepares the way for Biff's disastrous failure. By harping upon Uncle Ben's rapid rise to fortune, he builds in both boys a distaste for the type of regular, fairly routine work that will not make anyone, as Biff says, a "big shot boss in two weeks." Finally, by encouraging them to idolize him through his blown-up accounts of their situation, he does little to help them mature. Toward the end, Biff seems to be groping sadly toward some measure of self-knowledge, but Happy is still determined to "beat this racket" and come out "number one man." On the day of the big game, Charley ruefully asks Willy when he is going to grow up. In some ways Willy never does. His boyish enthusiasm is part of his appeal, but his persistent refusal to face facts squarely drives him at last to a violent death. Ironically, his suicide, to him the ultimate in magnificent gestures, merely leaves Linda woefully bereft and Biff more than ever sure that "he had the wrong dreams. All, all wrong."

BIFF LOMAN

At thirty-four, this husky, good-looking former star athlete is a moody, troubled man. Like Willy, he is worried both about family tensions and his work. He is fond of his mother and saddened to see her looking older. Even though he has never regained his idolizing reverence for Willy, he would very much like to meet him again on pleasant, amicable terms. In all probability he also misses the high praise with which Willy bolstered his self-confidence. Now, however, whenever he returns, obviously no success, he dreads his father's disapproval and is clearly on the defensive. Thus, when Willy "mocks" him and accuses him of failing out of spite, he is ready with an angry rejoinder. This, in turn, makes Linda antagonistic, and Biff, feeling guilty and inept, is more depressed than ever.

Having relied apparently too much in boyhood years upon the heady encouragement of an adored and adoring father, Biff seems never to have recovered fully from the Boston disillusionment. Bernard's account of Biff's burning his "University of Virginia" sneakers suggests the dramatic finality of Biff's renunciation of all bright college plans. After that he takes various short courses but always loses heart. The ranch work, on the other hand, does give him some satisfaction. Away from his father's disappointed frowning, he likes the chance to use his physical strength in the open air.

Yet he makes very little money at such seasonal jobs, and

keeps moving from one to another hoping for more. All the while, too, he cannot shake off his father's prediction of an extraordinarily great future for him. Trying better paying city work, he feels stifled by the routine and becomes impatient at the slowness of the rise to some position of security and respect. So he steals and runs off, engages in devising fantasy schemes for making a quick fortune, then drifts back to another dollar-an-hour cattle-herding stopgap. Even though this erratic program has left him increasingly anxious and disheartened, there is at least a faint hope for him. For Biff, at least, knows that he is "mixed-up" and wants to stop acting "like a boy." After his disastrous attempt to see Oliver, he does face bravely a few more harsh facts about his limitations and resolves to give up following the old "phony dream."

Actually, Biff, like Willy, tends to go to extremes. So his passionate insistence, toward the end, that he is "nothing," or that he and his father are both "a dime a dozen," still sounds a little like the uncompromising disclaimer of the youngster who had sobbingly burned his sneakers. Now he sees his father's dreams as "All, all wrong." Yet although he still talks a little like the grandstand hero, he is now groping toward a more realistic, more mature self-appraisal. Neither Willy nor Happy ever gets even that far.

LINDA LOMAN

Linda is primarily wife rather than mother. If she is motherly, her ministrations are for Willy rather than her sons. Except when it becomes necessary for her to remind him of unpaid bills, she is forever soothing him, flattering him, tactfully suggesting courses of action, and trying to get him to eat enough and get some rest. She is almost always patient and kind to him, ignoring his minor outbursts and considerately accepting without demur such obvious deceptions as the borrowing from Charley. Linda loves her husband, respects him as a steady, hard-working man, and regards his sufferings with compassion. But she humors him as a child rather than meeting him squarely as an adult.

Yet the same mild-mannered, gentle Linda can be surprisingly blunt and harsh when she talks to her sons. She may not ever challenge Willy's grandiose talk to his face, but she reveals a clear, tough-minded recognition of their true financial picture. She rebukes Biff for failing to keep in touch and orders him either to behave pleasantly to his father or to leave. She coolly describes Happy as a "philandering bum." After the restaurant disaster, she denounces both her sons fiercely, flings away their flowers and imperiously orders them out of the house. Except when they disturb or irritate Willy, she talks to them amiably enough. But she is simply not concerned about them. Her one thought is Willy. If their presence cheers him or helps him in some way, she is glad to have them around. But if what they do further upsets her already disturbed grown-up "child," then the sons must go and not return.

HAPPY LOMAN

This dashing "assistant to the assistant" buyer shares with Biff a fondness for rugged outdoor living but wants material success even more. He appears at first to have come to terms with life better than either his father or his brother. He has his own car and his own apartment. He has had considerable proof of his virile appeal to women, and has developed a glib line with which to impress them. In a small way, he is quite an accomplished liar and has all but convinced himself that he is slated to become the store's next merchandise manager.

Actually, he is by no means as well adjusted as he seems. For one thing, he cannot quiet his own scruples. He knows that he is wrong when he takes bribes, and he has some sense of guilt regarding the seduction of other men's fiancées. In addition, he does appreciate the fact that the merchandise manager, whose success he so patently envies, is still discontented and restless. So he suspects that even reaching that pinnacle may not guarantee happiness. Moreover, like Biff, he feels indoor work confining. Also physically strong, he misses the exaltation of the athletic contest, and has a certain contempt for the weaklings with whom he must work.

Happy still has vestiges of old ideals. He objects to all that is false around him, although he is false himself. Even while picking up a prostitute, he remarks what a shame it is that there are so few good women. He dreams of settling down with a decent girl like his mother. Although embarrassed by his father's odd behavior, he is not ungenerous. He did send Willy to Florida for a rest. He is genuinely fond of Biff.

Yet he often refuses to face unpleasant truths and resists Biff's attempts to clear up misconceptions as bitterly as Willy does. Whatever occasional admissions he makes, he will not give up either his dream world or his shabby sexual affairs. He may talk of changing his ways and getting married, but he never sounds convincing. His final act is to reject Biff's invitation to start anew, preferring to justify Willy's dream of coming out "number-one man." Unlike Biff, Happy learns relatively little from witnessing his father's collapse.

CHARLEY AND BERNARD

These good neighbors contrast strikingly to the Lomans. Unlike Willy, Charley lays no claim to greatness. He goes along calmly and quietly, undistinguished but relatively content. His salvation, he declares, is that he never took any interest in anything. That, of course, is not literally true for he shows unusually generous consideration of Willy. He set himself a modest goal and is satisfied with modest achievements.

Bernard is no match physically for the athletic Loman boys, and neither he nor his father can work so well with their hands. Bernard, however, studies hard, gets good grades, and despite Willy's disparaging predictions is clearly forging ahead brilliantly. At the time of Willy's breakdown, he has a wife and two sons and is pleading a big law case before the Supreme Court in Washington. When Willy observes wonderingly that Bernard does not brag, Charley says that his son does not have to because his deeds speak for themselves.

Curiously enough, although opposite in temperament to the Lomans, Charley and Bernard cannot help admiring them. Bernard has no illusions as to the foolishness of Biff's neglect of math, yet he tries constantly to be of help to him and pleads to carry his helmet or shoulder guards on the day of the big game. Charley, on his part, takes issue with Willy on such vital matters as the importance of being "well liked." Yet it is he who in the end defends Willy to Biff in almost rhapsodic terms. Willy sneered at Charley, insulted him, and then borrowed sizable sums from him, but Charley can say with vehemence, "Nobody dast blame this man."

DEATH OF A SALESMAN COMMENTARY

ESTABLISHED FAME

If *All My Sons* signaled the arrival of Arthur Miller as a most promising young playwright, *Death of a Salesman* raised him to the rank of major American dramatist. Appearing in 1949, two years after *All My Sons*, *Death of a Salesman* won the Pulitzer Prize, the Drama Critic's Circle Award, plus quite a few other awards. The esteemed New York *Times* drama critic Brooks Atkinson called *Death of a Salesman* "one of the finest dramas in the whole range of the American theater." Other leading writers also bestowed high praise. John Gassner saw it as "one of the triumphs of the mundane American stage." Gilbert W. Gabriel described it as a "fine thing, finely done," and Euphemia Wyatt termed it a "great American tragedy."

SOCIAL CRITICISM

The play takes issue with those in America who place too much stress upon material gain, at the expense of more admirable human values. There are, for instance, several angry comments on the company's callous disregard for Willy's welfare. Linda speaks with anger of his being taken off salary, and both boys think this an outrage. Biff later talks of his father as having "landed in the ash can" and suggests that this is all that a "hard-working drummer" can expect. But the most scathing indictment is actually delivered by means of the portrayal of Howard in the office scene. Howard is so engrossed in his new toy, the tape recorder, that he cannot pay much attention to the human being, Willy. His brusqueness, his impatience, and then his coldly unconcerned notice of dismissal support Willy's own contention that the business world has lost all respect, comradeship, and gratitude, and is now merely "cut and dried." The picture, as so often in Miller plays, is not wholly bleak. Charley, after all, is a fairly successful businessman who behaves very generously. But Willy's dismissal is still a harsh commentary on all who think of workers only as income-producing machines, those who, as Willy says, will "eat the orange and throw the peel away."

Yet there is also a more general criticism of American values. Willy loves his sons and wants what is best for them. His one insistent message to them is that they must rise rapidly in the business world, outshine all others, and be satisfied only with a fortune like Uncle Ben's. In the first place, there is no guarantee that mere wealth and high position would be rewarding. Happy's merchandise manager is clearly not ecstatic even with fifty-two thousand a year, a very good annual income in 1949. Apart from this, however, there is no indication that either the Loman boys or their father possess the skills necessary to command that kind of return. This combination of an unfeasible objective and limited talents leads to unfortunate consequences. Rather than be forced to endure the stigma of failure, all three constantly lie about their achievements. But the bragging never wholly covers their feelings of inadequacy. Their second escape route is to dream up dazzling get-rich-quick schemes and coast for a while on the glorious prospects. Yet sooner or later, such bubbles inevitably burst.

In addition, this undue concern over material success breaks down the bonds between men that form the basis for a smooth-functioning society. Arthur Miller develops as a major theme in many of his dramas the need for a greater sense of mutual responsibility. But when the one desirable goal is to get ahead of everybody else, then the spirit of helpfulness declines. Happy regards his fellow employees as "common" and "petty" or "pompous" and "self-important," and proceeds to ruin their fiancées. Accurately or otherwise, he suggests that this type of discreditable behavior may result from "an overdeveloped sense of competition." What Biff hated most about the business world was always having "to get ahead of the next fella." Ben's lesson to Biff about never fighting fair in the jungle thus seems curiously appropriate. We note that Willy always finds it necessary to disparage Charley and Bernard, possibly, as Charley suggests, because he has always been jealous. Miller implies that Americans place too much emphasis upon money-making as the one criterion of a man's worth.

Miller directs a third criticism against our tendency to play up the superficial. This is brought out by the excessive fuss over the football game. Charley asks Willy, who is rushing around with pennants, when he is going to grow up. The question implies a criticism of American society as a whole. Then there is Howard's playing with his tape recorder, a gadget that so fascinates him now that he is ready to throw out his camera, bandsaw, and other toys. In like manner in the restaurant scene the talk is of French champagne, magazine cover girls, pro-football stardom—commonplace and superficial American concerns. To Willy, people who play tennis and have a swimming pool are "fine people," without question. In Miller's opinion, a society so given to frivolous values and judgments reveals distorted values.

POLITICAL BEARINGS

The United States is an industrial nation, and its economic system is based on free enterprise and considerable competition. Some of those who are proud of the American way of life object to the criticism leveled against it in *Death of a Salesman*. Showing a "little man" like Willy so callously discharged after long years of service attacks the whole system. Several arguments have been advanced in opposition to this viewpoint. First of all, Willy himself is hardly represented as completely typical. Arthur Miller once noted that average men don't commit suicide. Secondly, Willy is not altogether an innocent victim. Part of his difficulty results from family tensions rather than defects in the system. Thirdly, the system seems to operate fairly enough for Charley and Bernard, both of whom are sympathetic characters. Finally, there is never any suggestion that some other existing system would be preferable, nor is Willy's downfall linked with some readily identifiable policy of some party or group. Miller is an intellectual much concerned about what he regards as certain defects in our society. *Death of a Salesman* has general political implications, but does not contain explicit social or political criticisms.

MODERN TRAGEDY

Death of a Salesman deals with middle-class people in a realistic setting. The salesman's house is in Brooklyn, and the big game takes place at Ebbets Field. The Lomans have owned a Studebaker and a Chevrolet, and wish they had bought a General Electric refrigerator. The restaurant is on West 48th Street, and Happy boasts that Biff is a quarterback with the New York Giants.

This is a play about a man's death. From the beginning, tragedy has dealt with death. Yet most early tragedies included a great reversal of fortunes, in which a great or powerful person fell to his ruin from a high position of wealth and authority. But at the start of the play, Willy is already broken. Further, he was never an influential or famous individual. Even the loyal Linda admits that he has never been a "great man" or even the "finest" of characters. Nevertheless, she maintains that he is worthy of some attention as a human being who suffers. After all, "a small man can be just as exhausted as a great man."

Willy, for all this ordinariness, has rather lofty aspirations for himself and his sons. His goals may not be altogether admirable. But, then, were those of Macbeth and such tyrant heroes of earlier tragedies? Yet Willy pursues his goals with passionate intensity. He seeks his concept of success with a terrible earnestness and even dies in quest of his dream. Viewed in one way, Willy is a pathetic, incompetent old drummer with absurd pretensions. Miller sees him, however, as aiming high and agonizing deeply. Hence, the "fall" of even such a poor, debt-ridden man can have genuine tragic aspects.

If the play thus contains a new type of tragic statement, it is also curiously lyrical in tone. While this is not poetic drama in the old sense, the preoccupation with the past often gives it a nostalgic, or elegiac, quality. All the Lomans look back a little sadly to happier days of untroubled comradeship when Willy capably directed his sons in carpentry projects for the home. Willy can remember, too, when the business world had in it an element of respect and gratitude. He can look further back to wagon trips through the developing West. There once was a time, too, when the little house was not jammed in among tall apartment buildings and when Biff waved to Willy from the football field, a young Hercules with the sun all around him. The delicate flute music and the leafy green effect of the lights upon the "fragile-seeming" house further add to the lyrical effect. *Death of a Salesman* is thus not only a drama of social criticism and a modern tragedy but also a mood piece, wistfully looking back.

EXPERIMENTAL FORM

As contrasted with *All My Sons,* this play has a much more creative and original format. Miller is attempting to recreate what goes on in Willy's troubled mind. He once thought of calling the play "The Inside of His Head," and having all scenes played behind a thin curtain, or scrim. Although this proposal was abandoned as unfeasible, the action does move easily back and forth from past to present. Yet, unlike mere accounts of the past, the flashbacks are part of the present action. When the distracted Willy is reminded of the disastrous Boston episode, he relives it, goes through it again, and this new, decidedly present experience adds to his current difficulties. When he holds a double conversation with Ben from the past and Charley in the present, it is all part of what is going on in his mind now. In general, this startling technique was very much admired. According to Miller, it was also imitated, usually by those who had no real grasp of its proper use. It is also interesting that the playwright returned to more conventional forms in subsequent works, only to revive this method in modified form in *After the Fall* in 1965.

CHARACTERISTIC THEMES

SELF-DESTRUCTION
The leading character meets a violent death by his own hands.

EXCESSIVE PERSONAL INVOLVEMENT
In *Death of a Salesman,* Willy and his sons are concerned about each other's actions to an extreme degree. Biff's discovery of his father's secret love affair puts an end to all of Biff's college ambitions. Willy's yearning for Biff's success finally helps motivate his suicide.

UNETHICAL PRACTICES
Willy countenances Biff's cheating on exams and stealing the football, passing such actions off as examples of initiative.

NEED FOR INTEGRITY
Biff tries to make Willy recognize how much has been false in their lives so that both may make a new start.

ESSAY QUESTIONS AND ANSWERS

QUESTION
Much of *Death of a Salesman* deals with the relationship between Willy and Biff. Could Happy have been eliminated?

ANSWER
No, for Happy is useful in providing a perspective by which the other two characters can be more accurately evaluated. Happy is reasonably open-handed. He will treat his father to dinner, even send him to Florida, and pledge more, if necessary. But he was never the favorite and was never caught up in Biff's terrible disillusioning experience. Except in a general fashion, Willy never seems to have expected much from this younger son. Yet Happy has learned from his father. He has been taught the need to push to the top, of sneering at superiors and coworkers, and of not being scrupulous about unethical practices. He is also an expert at bluffing, and lies almost instinctively whenever unpleasant truths threaten to prove irksome. Being harder than Willy and Biff, he has been able to work out a somewhat more satisfactory compromise. He has, after all, his car, his apartment, and his women friends, whereas both his father and his brother have almost no funds. He does have twinges of conscience but lets no troublesome sense of guilt interfere with his sexual pleasures. When Biff brings up some agonizing truths, Happy angrily denies them, preferring the tried and serviceable lie. Willy and Biff are more poetic, more romantic, more akin to the old visionary pioneers. They love more and suffer more. Happy has taken the worst of Willy's precepts and made them his life's code. As a character, he enables us to see Willy's errors in action. He also makes us appreciate the greater moral sensitivity of the other two Loman men.

QUESTION
If Willy is foolish and headstrong, are we to assume that Charley and Bernard represent the playwright's ideal?

ANSWER

Certainly Charley and Bernard seem to have more serene, more comfortable lives than the Lomans. Bernard has a wife and two sons, and his career is obviously thriving. His father can afford to lend Willy substantial sums, to have his own secretary, and to present a bottle of bourbon to his son. Charley can offer Willy a job. Moreover, the relationship between this father and son is friendly and untroubled. Hence, almost no negative side can be seen to their lives. By inference, the Lomans would be happier and more successful if they were able to conform to the steadier, more easy-going life patterns of their neighbors.

Yet there is something heroic in the Lomans' aspirations. Willy speaks of his father as an "adventurous man" and talks of a "little streak of self-reliance" in his family. Willy may be born in the wrong era for his type of skills, but he does have some vestiges of the old pioneering vision, the boundless optimism, the reckless element that was part of America's heritage. Why does Charley keep coming around despite the insults? Why does young Bernard slave patiently for Biff? Neither can or will adopt the Lomans' dangerous course, but both sense here a bit of excitement, a flash of glory absent in their well-regulated lives. Like most of the reckless heroes of other eras, the Lomans live more perilously and risk more. But even failing, they are the dreamers that rescue civilization from becoming too drearily cut and dried.

QUESTION

What dramatic purpose is served by using flashbacks instead of relating events in strict chronological order?

ANSWER

Ordinarily the flashback device is used primarily for exposition, that is, to convey background information needed to make the story as a whole intelligible. Of course, the scenes from the past in this play do indeed fulfill such a purpose.

The episode in the Boston hotel, for instance, explains the rift between Willy and Biff and accounts for Willy's sense of guilt. Yet such episodes also serve here another, more subtle purpose.

Willy Loman will kill himself because painful memories, guilt feelings, and various frustrations combine to unsettle his mind and distort his thinking. The flashbacks here are scenes from the past that torment and confuse Willy in the present. Pleasant recollections make him more agonizingly conscious of current sorrows. Disturbing ones reinforce the anxieties of the moment. Used in this fashion, episodes from Willy's past are very much a part of his later experience and, in a way, are just as essential to the main action as his crucial final encounters with Howard and Biff.

Finally, since this is to some extent a psychological drama, what Willy's confused mind instinctively recalls tells us a great deal about the kind of man he is. For instance, would Charley remember the football game so vividly? Thus the flashbacks here not only provide exposition but advance the plot and reveal character traits.

QUESTION
Why is Willy Loman an unusual choice for a tragic hero?

ANSWER
Tragedy was first successfully developed by the ancient Greek playwrights as Aeschylus, Sophocles, and Euripides. Many of our traditional concepts of tragedy derive from their handling of the form and from the commentary on their works provided by the philosopher Aristotle. The Greek tragic hero was quite different from Willy Loman.

First of all, the Greek hero was usually a rich, well-born, successful man. Oedipus, for instance, is the rich and respected ruler of a state, enjoying good health, peace of mind, and the contentment of a satisfactory home life. By contrast, Willy starts as a broken, exhausted, confused "little man," bitterly at odds with his eldest son. The Greek hero fell from an exalted position, and much of the tragedy consisted in the appalling extent of his decline. But Willy never has far to fall.

Secondly, the Greek hero, although not a perfect man, seemed to sum up man's nobler aspirations. Some have felt that Willy's values are so warped and his vision so limited that he cannot qualify as a noble example of mankind. The lordly warrior Agamemnon, they maintain, would not fret about being "well liked" or get so worked up over a football game. To this Arthur Miller has replied that even a poor, confused man can want distinction for himself and his son, and that if he wants it enough to die for it, he achieves tragic status. Not everyone has accepted Miller's contention, but some agree that since our civilization is not ancient Greece, our tragic heroes will perhaps differ too.

QUESTION
What purposes are served by the flute music used throughout *Death of a Salesman?*

ANSWER
From the first the flute is used to create a mood. Even though Willy is an aging man, lumbering in with weighty valises, he is also an individual forever pursuing an elusive vision. The flute music keeps this side of Willy before the audience.

It also provides transitions from present-day scenes to flashbacks and vice versa. Unlike many more conventional works, this play does not lower the curtain as the action moves from one place to the other, or even from one moment in time to another. Instead, the flute smooths over the frequent shifts and helps set successive scenes.

Thirdly, the flute is connected with Willy's family history. His father, that great, "wild-hearted" man, made flutes and took his family in a wagon all over the country selling them. He was thus a craftsman, and Willy is always proud of being able to do things with his hands. He was also, of course, a salesman, and his roving, "adventurous" life has obviously signified to Willy a type of free, unencumbered existence, with profits unlimited for those who can quickly invent some such clever gadget. The sound of the flute is thus also the call that summons Willy to a nomadic career, probably in the great West.

QUESTION

How does *Death of a Salesman* criticize contemporary American society?

ANSWER

The play suggests that modern business is so coldly competitive that decent human values are ignored. Willy gives many years of steady service to the Wagner Company. As soon as his production begins to decline, he is taken off salary and put back on straight commission. Later, he is discharged, apparently without any pension. In addition, both Biff and Happy talk of business conditions in terms that suggest that competition encourages sharp practices or outright dishonesty.

The play also takes issue with exaggerated emphasis upon personal charm rather than upon more solid character traits. Willy keeps telling Biff that it is all important to be well liked. Biff can fail subjects and even steal with impunity provided that he has a winning smile and an attractive manner. Actually, Biff's poor grades deprive him of scholarships and because of his lack of other necessary skills he never makes high wages. Despite his likable personality, theft still draws him a jail term.

Finally, the drama hints that too much stress on the importance of certain types of white-collar work has driven those into it who would be better off working with their hands. In general, the overall worship of material success is seen to produce in some instances little more than a sense of failure and frustration.

QUESTION
Why does Charley once remark that Willy really is a salesman and does not know it?

ANSWER
So far as Willy's actual achievements as a representative for the Wagner Company are concerned, it is hard to evaluate his record. Linda tends to flatter him, Howard is too ready to deny all his claims, and Willy himself rarely offers reliable facts about his work. Chances are, however, that at least in his prime, Willy was as good as the next man. He has, after all, held the job over three decades. He does support his family except for the final few months.

However ordinary or average his work may be, Willy is an expert at "selling" himself certain dubious notions. He is forever bragging about his popularity in New England and seems convinced that many people will come from other states to his funeral. He is certain that Biff, having played a good game of football, will outshine everyone in the business world. Later he is certain that Oliver will lend Biff a sizable sum although his son can offer no security. At the end, he talks himself into the belief that his suicide will somehow enable Biff to take the lead once more from Bernard and become "magnificent." Charley's wry comment in the "Requiem," seems to take into account the astonishing facility Willy has for persuading himself and even others to buy unlikely possibilities.

BIBLIOGRAPHY

ARTHUR MILLER'S PLAYS

After the Fall. New York: Bantam Books, 1965. (Paperback.)

All My Sons, in *Six Great Modern Plays.* New York: Dell, 1956. (Paperback.) Also in *Collected Plays.*

The American Clock. New York: Dramatists Play Service, 1985. (Orig. published 1980.).\

The Archbishop's Ceiling. New York: Dramatists Play Service, 1985; Grove Press, 1988, (Orig. published 1977.).\

Collected Plays. New York: The Viking Press, 1958. (Includes *All My Sons, Death of a Salesman, The Crucible, A Memory of Two Mondays,* and *A View from the Bridge.* Also a long, detailed, and helpful Introduction by the playwright.)

The Creation of the World and Other Business, 1972.

The Crucible. New York: The Viking Press, 1953; Also New York: Bantam Books, 1963. (Paperback.) And in *Collected Plays.*

Danger, Memory. New York: Grove Press, 1987.

Death of a Salesman. New York: The Viking Press, 1964. (Paperback.) Also in *Collected Plays.*

Elegy for a Lady. New York: Dramatists Play Service, 1982.

An Enemy of the People. Adapted from Ibsen. New York: The Viking Press, 1951.

Incident at Vichy. New York: The Viking Press, 1965. (Paperback.)

The Last Yankee. New York: Viking Penguin, 1994.

The Man Who Had All the Luck, in *Cross-Section,* ed. E. Seaver. New York: A.A. Wyn, Inc., 1944.

A Memory of Two Mondays, in *Collected Plays*; and with *A View from the Bridge.* New York: The Viking Press, 1955.

The Misfits. Screenplay, 1961.

The Price. New York: Viking Penguin, 1988. (Orig. published by Dramatists Play Service, 1968.)

The Ride Down Mt. Morgan. New York: Viking Penguin, 1992.

Some Kind of Love Story. New York: Dramatists Play Service, 1983.

Up From Paradise, 1974.

A View from the Bridge, in *Collected* Plays. New York: The Viking Press, 1955.

CRITICISM

Adam, Julie. *Versions of Heroism in Modern American Drama: Redefinitions by Miller, Williams, O'Neill, and Anderson,* 1991.

Approaches to Teaching Arthur Miller's Death of a Salesman. New York: Modern Language Association of America, 1995.

Arthur Miller. New York: Chelsea House Publishers, 1987.

Arthur Miller's Death of a Salesman. New York: Chelsea House Publishers, 1988.

Bentley, Eric. *In Search of Theater.* New York: Alfred A. Knopf, 1953.

Bloom, Harold. *Willy Loman.* New York: Chelsea House, 1991.

Carson, Neil. *Arthur Miller.* New York: St. Martins Press, 1988.

Dukore, Bernard Frank. *Death of a Salesman and The Crucible.* Atlantic Highlands, New Jersey: Humanities Press International, 1989.

Gassner, John. *The Theatre in Our Times.* New York: Crown Publishers, Inc., 1955

Glassman, Bruce. *Arthur Miller.* Englewood Cliffs, New Jersey: Silver Burdett Press, 1990.

Heiney, Donald. *Recent American Literature.* New York: Barron's Educational Series, 1958.

Krutch, Joseph Wood. *American Drama Since 1918.* New York: G. Braziller, 1957.

Moss, Leonard. *Arthur Miller.* Boston: G. K. Hall, 1987.

Schlueter, June. *Arthur Miller*. New York: Ungar, 1987.

Welland, Dennis. *Miller, the Playwright*. New York: Methuen, 1985.